The Greatest People
I Never Knew

A Funeral Director's lessons about people he came to know only in death, and how they changed his life

By

Eric M. Daniels

ISBN: 1-4140-1190-3 (e-book)
ISBN: 1-4140-1189-X (Paperback)

This book is printed on acid free paper.

Book designed and edited by Robin Stamm

Photo credit: Photography by Nylora, Concord, NH

1stBooks – rev. 11/06/03

Reader Reviews

"As funeral directors, we see so many sides of life and each life is unique of itself. This book shows that there are many remarkable people around us. We just need to look and listen."
— Frances O'Connell, Miami, Florida

"Your book is very well written and very moving. I feel like I know all the people in the stories."
— Barbara Pate, York, Pennsylvania

"This book is incredibly moving. I found myself crying one minute and laughing the next. I highly recommend it to everyone."
— Sheryl Coombs, Concord, New Hampshire

"After losing my husband, reading this book has helped me to accept life as God has given it to me. It's the most meaningful and inspirational book I've ever read."
— Shirley Stewart, Devils Lake, North Dakota

"You have such a gift of sensitivity and an awareness of what is so truly important in life. Thank you for sharing your experiences with me."
— Ellen McDonnell, Wakefield, Massachusetts

"Your book shows what's important in life, and what's not. It reaffirms that our real heroes are in our own back yards."
— Eric Solter, Anaheim, California

"I have presented this book to many friends and family members who are struggling with the grieving process. Mr. Daniels, through his book, has provided a great deal of comfort."
— Auddie Cox, Colorado Springs, Colorado

"Let us endeavor so to live that when we come to die, even the undertaker will be sorry."

— Mark Twain

Foreword

FOR THOSE OF us who live on, death teaches us many things. It teaches us that life is indeed brief and that we must strive to enjoy it while we're here. It teaches us not to worry so much about the little things. It teaches us that kindness is what really matters. And it teaches us to look for and acknowledge the unique and very special gifts of each individual—before it's too late. This book is about acknowledging the gifts of thirteen unique individuals who, in death, touched the life of Funeral Director Eric Daniels. Their remembered lives and their deaths taught him many important lessons— lessons you, too, can learn simply by reading this poignant book.

For many years now—ever since my eight-year apprenticeship in a funeral home when I was a young adult—I have been a proponent of funerals. In today's "death-free" culture, we are forgetting the importance of funerals. The funeral ritual, too, is a public, traditional, and symbolic means of expressing our beliefs, thoughts, and feelings about the death of someone loved. Rich in history and rife with symbolism, the funeral ceremony helps us acknowledge the reality of the death, gives testimony to the life of the deceased, encourages the expression of grief in a way consistent with the culture's values, provides support to mourners, allows for the embracing of faith and beliefs about life and death, and offers continuity and hope for the living.

Alan D. Wolfelt, Ph.D.
Author of *Creating Meaningful Funeral Ceremonies:
A Guide for Families*
and many books on healing and grief
Director of Center for Loss and Life Transition,
Fort Collins, Colorado

Acknowledgments

I'D LIKE TO thank the following people for helping bring this book to fruition:

Funeral Directors Ben Brodeur, Patricia Kolski, Ronald Albury, Dennis Daulton, Ralph Covert, Darwin Gearhart, Jim Heffner, Ernie Heffner, John Katora, Cary Troxel, and Joe Walker for being outstanding examples of leadership and for giving me the inspiration to be the best. Jerry Bellew, for pointing me in the right direction. Mr. Robert Bennett, the finest Funeral Director I know, and a man I strive to emulate every day. My coworkers Mike Bales, Terry Jelley, Bruce Currier, Jeromy Heeter, Jamie Jackter, Rob Chase, and the late Dominick Susi — the best coworkers one could hope for. Janis Taylor and Glenn Tekerman for the long hours spent putting my notes in an orderly fashion and for being the kind of friends everyone wants to have. Robin Stamm for her expert advice, critical editing, flexibility and generosity. Dr. Alan Wolfelt for his time, graciousness, and contribution to this book and the funeral profession. The Miami-Dade Community College and the W.L. Philbrick School of Funeral Sciences for giving me a solid foundation and the best funeral service education in the country. My children: Jessica, Stefanie, Joey, Ashley and Megan; and my adopted nephews Matt and Josh, for putting up with me. And, of course, my wife Kelly — without her love, support and encouragement I would never have started this project, let alone finished it.

Finally, I owe a deep debt of gratitude to the families connected with these stories, since it was through them that I came to know their loss, as well as the extraordinary character of the person they continue to honor. It is their love and input that brings this book to life and seals the memory of their loved ones.

"If someone so great once was,
then someone so great will always be."
— Max Kane
"The Mighty"

Dedicated to my maternal grandfather
Charles J. Kenney (1904 – 1985)
and
My paternal grandmother
Florine A. (Francesco) Daniels (1917 – 2000)

The greatest people I ever knew.

BECAUSE THIS BOOK tells the stories of people I never really knew (although I did meet two of them), it wasn't possible to include the stories of the wonderful people I *have* known who are no longer with us. These people have inspired me, just as the people in each of the following chapters have impacted my life. For this reason, I include their names as a secondary "dedication", and will always carry their story in my heart.

Nick Manning, DMD
Deputy Fire Chief James McDonnell
Raymond M. Daniels, Jr.
Jim Humphries
Phoebe Kenney
Thomas O'Connor
Mason Blake
Virginia Wells
Rhoda Fix
Henry Eager
Alan Everson
Dominick Susi

Prologue

WHEN YOU'RE A Funeral Director, you learn that above all else, life is about people — not money, not prestige, not fame; it's people and how they interact with those around them. When you learn about a person after their life is over, you find out what kind of person they were; whether they helped their neighbors, or were there for strangers, or if they sacrificed themselves to do what they felt would make the world a better place.

The stories in this book are about a few of the people I've met only through their death. Since I'm a Funeral Director in Concord, New Hampshire, these people are from the communities surrounding Concord. And they are people who made a lasting impact on me because of the difference they made in the lives of others — the people I would come to know in the course of doing my job. The experiences I've had are impossible to explain. I can, however, share what I've heard.

The following stories are about ordinary people who lived extraordinary lives. They are representative of the kind of people who positively affect my thought processes, my values, and my understanding of a full and well lived life.

It's my hope these stories, and my reactions to them, will help do the same for you.

Table of Contents

It's a Wonderful Life

The Story of Edward (Ebbie) Nemiccolo
1926 - 1999
"The miracle is this — the more we share, the more we have."
Leonard Nimoy

I HAD ACTUALLY MET Ebbie myself once at (of all places) a funeral. Ebbie and his wife had sat in the middle pews waiting for the service to begin and I happened to notice they didn't have memorial folders—which are traditionally given to everyone who attends a funeral. As I handed them  their folders, I saw Ebbie's eyes twinkle when he smiled. With those eyes, he thanked me and I thought "gee, he not only *looks* like Santa, he acts like him!"

Two weeks later, Ebbie was diagnosed with an aneurysm of the brain, and he died two weeks after that.

When Ebbie died, his four grown daughters were gathered around his bed and, when they realized he was gone, they layed their heads on his chest and cried. After a while, one of the girls went and got four glasses and a bottle of wine and they each toasted their father, with expressions of how much he'd meant to them. And then they called me.

I got the call at 1:30 a.m. on a cold December night. We arrived at the Nemiccolo home within the hour and soon brought Ebbie to the funeral home.

The next morning, Ebbie's widow, Shirley, together with all his children, came to the funeral home to make arrangements for a visitation and a church service. I was soon to learn we were dealing with a very unique man. The family wanted his Santa Claus outfit (which had been made by his daughters) to be placed in the casket with him. Of course we'd do that. And, since it was obvious

1

he was special, I suggested the family bring mementos to the visitation and the service as a way of telling Ebbie's story.

To my surprise, on the night of the viewing, they brought in 50 Santa Claus figurines — which was *half* of Ebbie's collection. The figurines had been given to Ebbie over the years by people who'd been touched by his kindness. There was also a collage of photos, complete with a picture of his truck with the license plate "Ho Ho Ho", telling the story of a man who'd lived a wonderful life.

When the viewing was over, more than 500 people had passed through the doors of the Bennett Funeral Home. With everyone gone, his children gathered around the casket, reminiscing as laughter mingled with tears. Each girl tried on his Santa hat and one even tried on his boots. Although I was an outsider, I felt the love they'd shared, even in Ebbie's death.

After he died, our local newspaper — The *Concord Monitor* — ran a front page article about Ebbie. The article reads:

Season of joy begins on sad note.
Nemiccolo, a dear friend to local children, dies
By Lisa Wangsness, *Concord Monitor* staff

Bow — A man who delighted hundreds of children each year by playing Santa Claus at schools, community organizations and private Christmas parties died early yesterday morning at his home.

With his natural snowy beard, gentle voice and kindly, attentive demeanor, Ed Nemiccolo was arguably the most sought after and adored Santa Claus in the area. His schedule for Christmas Eve was booked in July; schools made December appointments before school started.

"Kids in town knew him," said Shirley Nemiccolo, his wife of 48 years. "When he was out raking the leaves or piling wood, kids would holler out the school bus, 'Hi Santa!'"

"He really and truly felt God had given him his face and his hair and his personality to do good and make the world a better place," she said, adding her husband would have wanted to reassure children that the real Santa Claus lives on in people's hearts."

Nemiccolo was born in Dedham, Mass., and entered the Navy at age 17 to serve in World War II. When the war ended, he settled in New Hampshire, where he met his wife and began working as a house painter and carpenter. The couple raised four daughters and a son in Bow, where they lived for 44 years.

In 1976, Nemiccolo and some friends grew out their beards for the country's bicentennial celebration. The white beard prompted the state hospital, where he was working at the time, to ask him to play Santa Claus for patients.

As Nemiccolo told the Monitor in 1995, "I've been riding with Rudolph ever since."

By word-of-mouth, local groups and families began clamoring for visits from Bow's own Kris Kringle. Nemiccolo owned eight Santa suits, including a red velvet one his daughters made for him for his birthday. Before he retired, he always took the entire month of December off from work to squeeze in about 90 appearances at churches, hospitals, libraries, day care centers and family parties.

When he suffered a stroke in 1991, his wife took over the scheduling and drove him from place to place. On Christmas Eve, his daughters gave him a bag of snacks to tide him over as many as seven stops.

The Nemiccolo family, his wife said, never complained about his absence during the holidays, and let him relax with the newspaper when he needed "down" time between visits.

"He was always there on Christmas Day," Shirley Nemiccolo said.

Parents loved Nemiccolo not only for his extraordinary resemblance to the classic Kris Kringle but for the way he took care to spend plenty of time with each child, listening seriously as they whispered their Christmas wishes in his ear.

"He was just so gentle with the kids," said Andrea Amirault, the former president of the Concord Cooperative Play School. "He wasn't looking over at the parents when he was talking to the kids. He was just totally engrossed with them."

Marta Shibles, who lives in Chichester and whose family invited Nemiccolo to their Christmas Eve for 17 years, said the kids in her family looked forward all day to Santa's arrival and shrieked when he finally strode in with his bag full of presents.

"To my kids, this man was Santa — not Santa's helper, like everybody else — Santa Claus," Shibles said.

Nemiccolo got presents in return, too, Shirley Nemiccolo said. A miniature tree for all the ornaments children gave Santa had to be replaced recently by a full-sized tree.

The children in one Bow family fixed a special bag of crafts and baked goodies for Santa every year. And then there are the Santa sculptures.

"I venture to say we have about 100 (Santa) statues," she said. "Standing ones, little ones, big ones, fat ones, wooden ones."

Nemiccolo was gearing up for another hectic Christmas season when he suffered a stroke on Nov. 20; he never fully recovered.

He spent his last days at home with his wife and children. His 10 grandchildren and four great-grandchildren visited and cut paper snowflakes to hang in the windows. People called and came by to check in, their arms bursting with food for the family.

Yesterday, his wife looked out the window as a school bus passed.

"I saw all these little faces looking over here," she said.

(Reprinted with permission from the Concord Monitor)

The Nemiccolo family received over 500 cards and letters from people in the community, and some were from people Mrs. Nemiccolo didn't even know. She received a letter addressed to "Mrs. Santa Claus" from a fifth grade student named Brittany Verville. Brittany wrote:

"I was so sad when I found out that your husband had passed away. He was a kind man who made children happy and made people laugh and smile. He was loved very much by children and everyone else in Bow, N.H."

And Marcia Black wrote this:

My Husband and I live on Bow Bog Road and like many Bow residents have special memories of your husband. A recent one was very special to us. Our 3-year old granddaughter came to stay with us this summer. As we have never had a Christmas with her, we planned Christmas in August. This entailed a letter to Santa to ask permission to have a special Christmas in Bow and, of course, a proclamation from Santa okaying the day. It so happened that on the very day Santa was to come, I was driving into Concord with my granddaughter Alex when I saw Mr. Nemiccolo out on your lawn talking with a neighbor. I slowed down and told Alex to look. I will never forget the look on her tiny face as she said, "Grama, Santa is on vacation too!" I told her that must be why he said he would deliver presents to Bow that night. He knew he was going to be in Bow on vacation. We immediately then had to drive to Penacook so she could tell her Grandpa that she had seen Santa and he was wearing "jeans and a T shirt just like me." What a magical moment for her and for me.

I will always remember Mr. Nemiccolo reading "The Night Before Christmas" to my Brownie Troop and how beautiful his pictures were in the Brookstone Christmas Catalogue. Bow has truly been blessed to have our very own Santa.

These, and many other letters and comments, are how I came to know Ebbie. I learned he never asked for anything in return; not even for gas money for his "Santa trips" to schools, nursing homes and businesses. He was happy to simply give. What a pure approach to life!

Ebbie touched so many lives, he received more than one tribute in our local paper. This one was written by someone who knew "Santa" — and the gift of giving — in a very direct way.

A lifetime's gift: a kind heart, a warm touch and 79 cents
By Nancy Cieliczka, For the *Concord Monitor*

Years ago, there grew a beautiful 8-year old girl with light brown hair and soft hazel eyes. She was a Brownie and dressed one cold day in her crisp jumper and white blouse, beanie hat and green sash, which held the patches and badges from her short scouting career.

Her village gathered to celebrate the approach of the Christmas season, with skating on the town pond, s'mores and hot chocolate, lighting of the Christmas tree, singing and a simple but festive supper in the Bow community center.

All the town's scouts gathered to sell cookies, knickknacks and homemade crafts and trinkets to the very parents and families who had organized their efforts. The community's own Santa Claus was there to preside over the event.

Santa's long hair and beard were snow white year-round, even in the heat of the summer when he waved at passers-by while digging weeds in his garden. His overalls and T-shirts didn't conceal his identity, nor did the Santa borders that flew above his doorway and from tree branches.

At Christmas time his white hair and beard contrasted with his bright red suit and coal-black boots, and his girth and ruddy complexion confirmed that he was the only true St. Nicholas.

As Santa wandered through the community building chatting with children, he noticed the Brownie standing alone at a craft table, fingering a delicate gold-plated peacock ornament, encircled in a thin ring of the same gold plate. She put the decoration down and walked slowly away, but her eyes kept returning to it, and she inched back, touching it again.

Once more she counted the coins in her left hand, then sighed and moved away. Santa saw the disappointment on her face. He walked over to her, took her hand and led her back to the craft table.

"The peacock is lovely, isn't it?" he asked.

She nodded. "My mommy would think so, too, but I don't have enough money to buy it for her."

"Well, let me see," said Santa. "Let's count your coins again, just in case. We all make mistakes once in awhile."

When she reached the end of her counting, he continued for her, adding the 79 cents she needed for the purchase. Her back straightened, and she smiled and whispered, "Thank you, Santa."

She gave the money to the craft keeper, who wrapped the gold-plated peacock in tissue paper and put it in a small white box. The Brownie gingerly pushed her gift deep into her pocket and skipped away, a marvelous secret tucked in her heart.

She stopped, turned once to lock eyes with Santa, smiled and waved to him. He winked at her before moving on.

On Christmas morning, the little girl could scarcely wait for her gift to be unwrapped. She held her breath as her mother slid her fingers under the tape that held the wrinkled paper in place. Her mother held the ornament up to the window. Together they were transfixed by a brilliant ray of light that touched the peacock and made it glisten as it bobbed on its delicate gold ring.

The little girl broke the spell, exclaiming with bursting pride, "Isn't it beautiful! Santa helped me buy it for you, because I didn't have enough money."

Tears welled in the mother's eyes as she took the little girl in her arms and whispered thank you in her ear.

Together they placed the peacock on the Christmas tree and marveled at how fragile and shimmering it was. Indeed, it seemed to shine brighter than all the other decorations.

Every year after that, the peacock was placed on the tree with much ceremony and always with warm remembrance of Santa Claus.

The endless story:

The little girl turned 9, then 13, then 16. Far too soon, in the summer of the year, she graduated from high school and was about to move her belongings away to college. She had worked hard, saving her money for the supplies she would need.

One day, the grown child came home with a bouquet and a new $5 bill clutched in her hands. With purpose, she wrapped the flowers in pink tissue paper, placed the $5 bill in a pink envelope and said quietly, "I'm going to see Santa. Be back soon."

The story seems to have no ending, and it remains a mystery as to who was more richly blessed. Is it the little girl grown up, who always remembered Santa's kindness, carried the secret in her heart and drew from it as she helped a needy friend or acquaintance? Is it the mother who, every year as she touched the golden peacock, remembered Santa's compassion and generosity?

Or could Santa have been the richer, as he watched the light glow in that 8-year-old Brownie's eyes when she smiled and waved to him? Or as he remembered her yearly hugs at the community center? Or as she entered his home as a young woman and handed him flowers, tucked the $5 bill in his hand and kissed him gently on the cheek?

All that is certain is that he gave bits and pieces of that $5 to other village children, to begin the story again.

Although he lived modestly, it seems he had all the riches anyone could ask for because — to him — being rich meant making others happy.

7

The biggest lesson I learned from him is true altruism. If I had my druthers, I would prefer to touch as many lives as he did than to have a million dollars.

Take his example with you today as you go about your daily routine. Someone out there needs a smile, a wave, a hug, an ear to listen, or maybe even a quarter. We all have at least one talent we can share with the world. Share it and see what happens. Ebbie would suggest nothing less.

Our Little Moo and God's Eternal Angel

The Story of Zachary Ryan Crabtree
1995 – 1996

"When you are a mother, you are never really alone in your thoughts. A mother always has to think twice, once for herself and once for her child."
Sophia Loren

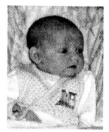

IN ALL MY years as a Funeral Director, I've been touched by many children, and Zachary Ryan Crabtree stands out in my mind. Sudden Infant Death Syndrome (SIDS) took 3-month old Zachary's life. But despite his infancy, he'd touched many lives, and that was obvious from the beginning.

I met his parents, Matthew and Cheryl, when they came to make his funeral arrangements. They'd brought *their* parents with them and we talked for some time. Naturally, it was upsetting and difficult for all of them. Still, I heard them say, time and again, how beautiful and happy Zachary had been. In fact, Cheryl said he loved balloons so much, she'd decided that, in lieu of flowers, she'd like people to send balloons to fill the entire funeral home...and that's what happened. During the viewing, the room was filled with balloons and memories of "Little Moo" (as Zach had come to be known) as "Winnie the Pooh" played on our sound system.

From a professional standpoint, all went smoothly, although behind the scenes, I was in the middle of a personal struggle. Due

9

to the nature and suddenness of his death, the law requires an autopsy be done to determine the cause of death. As part of that process, the hospital asked Zachary's parents if they would like to have his organs donated. Cheryl and Matthew agreed to donate anything that would benefit anyone, with the exception of his eyes, which were the most beautiful eyes they'd ever seen and they wanted Zachary to have them, even in death. When the autopsy was complete, I drove to the hospital to bring Zachary back to the Funeral Home.

It was difficult to embalm this child. He was truly an idyllically beautiful baby and that alone was enough to throw my concentration. But I also ran into problems. He was so tiny, his vessels were delicate and hard to find. And, since he'd been autopsied, I had to work on several separate areas. All this was compounded by my own emotions: I was struggling to understand why such an innocent beautiful child would die. It took me longer than it should have to prepare him for viewing.

Before I was finished, Cheryl asked me to check Zachary's eyes, since she wanted to be sure he still had them. She insisted that I be truthful with her if they were gone. I lifted his eyelids and found only cotton and my heart sank. I thought about lying to Cheryl to spare her additional grief but somehow, I felt (oddly) that Zachary wouldn't let me. It was as if he told me: "Tell her the truth and it will be okay." So I did, and it was.

Dr. James Filiano, a pediatrician who attended to Zachary, wrote this tribute:

Love and Duty

It does not matter what day or month I met Zachary. I was asked to write something about Zachary himself, but I can not. I can not because my memories are overwhelmed by a timeless message taught to me by mother and child together.

Zachary was a few months old and napping at the home of a trusted baby sitter. His mother arrived, saw him sleeping comfortably upstairs, and went down to visit with the adults for just a few moments. When she went back to awaken him, he was dead!

Can you feel the shock and terror and disbelief? This infant with the luscious puffy cheeks, the smiling eyes, the adorable little sounds, this long-awaited and much loved baby was gone! I am not an author who can describe how horrible the feeling must be for a mother. I can only ask the reader to visualize and live the moment. If you are like me, you will stop yourself just as the feeling gets too hard to bear. Something like this feeling was in Zachary's Mom as she ran down the stairs with the baby in her arms, shouting, asking for help, pleading with someone and something to take the terror away and bring her baby back.

He received CPR and recovered a pulse and blood pressure and he was brought to the hospital where I was in charge of the Pediatric Intensive Care Unit that day. I felt the way I usually do when this situation occurs: serious, focused, sad, angry, intense, lonely, and eager to muster all the resources we have to stabilize the child. If the baby's blood flow had stopped for only a minute, he might recover. We have seen that before, so we try to face this dismal situation with a bit of hope.

We also try to find the cause, and treat that if possible: Did he have an infection? a seizure? a brain abnormality? a biochemical problem? If so, we could treat those problems successfully. Our biggest fear was that he succumbed to Sudden Infant Death Syndrome.

During the course of our management, it became clear that Zachary would not recover, and eventually he died despite our full efforts. We then had to proceed with a very onerous task: we had to continue our pursuit of a cause, and this included an autopsy and a search for either an infectious disease that might affect other children he had contacted, a genetic disease that might affect his siblings, or child abuse.

I ask the reader again to take a moment and visualize this situation. An apparently healthy infant dies suddenly. If he was harboring a contagious disease, his siblings, his parents, or others at the baby sitter's may be in danger. If he was the victim of a genetic biochemical disease, one of his other siblings, or a future sibling, might be at risk for sudden death. If he died because he had been shaken, then other babies are at risk from the same perpetrator. Therefore, for the potential benefit of his family and other children, it was my duty, and the duty of the health care system of the state to find the cause. But imagine the shock and fury that a newly grieving parent feels when she recognizes that she is one potential suspect in a child abuse investigation! The reader must understand that the story we were told – Zachary was sleeping quietly upstairs – may have been true, but it also might have been false. How could we know? We were not present. We do not know the parents or the baby sitter's environment. In the situation of an untimely death, the State must assume anyone is a suspect. This is not viciousness. This is prudent neutrality. But to a parent, this is a repulsive insult.

I felt much of that revulsion when I told the parents what our duties were. It is a revulsion I feel whether or not I think child abuse is likely. All the nurses and physicians caring for Zachary doubted abuse, but knew we were obligated to pursue the possibility. All felt the same revulsion, but all felt the same sense of inescapable duty.

Zachary's mother was, indeed, shocked by the idea and the implied accusation. She responded negatively. But here is where I was taught an astounding, timeless, memorable lesson. Within a short time, Zachary's mother processed the entire issue. She saw the importance of the duty we had, and recognized its validity. Well before the diagnosis of Sudden Infant Death Syndrome was confirmed, and child abuse discarded, Zachary's mother...became an ally in the pursuit of a diagnosis. Since then, she has remained a supporter for Sudden Infant Death Syndrome and remains a compassionate parent.

I was amazed by Zachary's mother's courage through the process. That courage caused me to reflect on this matter many times over the years. I was a child of the late 60's. I doubted the establishment, especially after the dishonesty of McNamara and Nixon. Because of this doubt, as a teenager I developed a cautious distrust of the characteristic "duty to the establishment". To this day, I often doubt myself, because I am now part of "the establishment", just as I doubted over Zachary's case. I valued love as the highest virtue, and often thought that love and duty were often innately in conflict. Zachary's mother taught me otherwise. Her love for her child extended to a love for other children, and other potential victims. Her love drove her to overcome the insult we had added to her grief. Her love made her see that our duty was her duty, too: a duty to her son's memory, a duty to her other children, a duty to her husband, a duty to other infants, a duty to her community.

In the end, Zachary's mother taught me that love begets us all, and love begets duty. Love and duty, like mother and child, eventually can nourish and sustain each other, each in their own different ways. Zachary and his mother taught me that love and duty are not innately conflicting virtues. Psalm 85 implies much the same — that divinity is a state where "Love and duty meet; and Justice and Mercy will kiss." I think of Zachary and his mother often, and I hope the lesson they taught me...will remain in my heart and mind all my life: the lesson that love and duty are closely related virtues, as close as Mother and child.

We can only imagine the suffering a parent goes through after losing a child. Sometimes, however, we neglect to address the feeling of the grandparents. Zachary was the first grandchild for Nana and Papa Baum and Gramma and Grampa Crabtree. Gramma Crabtree said, "I kissed his soft pale cheek goodbye, but part of him stayed...His spirit will live forever." Grampa Crabtree described the sheer horror he experienced when he said, "I just could not accept the fact that this little boy who had never harmed anyone could be taken from us. In the parking lot at the Funeral Home the sun was shining and I told my wife Joan that I should be playing golf, not making plans to bury our grandson. I just hope no other parent or grandparent has to go through this. SIDS is inconsiderate and cruel."

Zachary's Eulogy was delivered by his Godparents, Rick and Anita on April 17, 1996:

Today we say goodbye to Zachary, remembering and cherishing his short time with us and the countless memories he brought us.

Zachary was a happy baby and will always know how much he is loved. He was many things to many people, a son, a grandson, a nephew, a godson, and a playmate. He was a ray of sunshine to everyone's life he touched. Even though Zachary was here for a short time, he was still his own little person, with an exceptional smile, a one-of-a-kind laugh, and a twinkle in his deep blue eyes. Like every baby, he loved to be held and talked to, but Zach especially liked the frequent "mile walks" through the house.

Those who knew Zachary will remember him as a sweet and precious baby. For those especially close to him, we will remember him as our "Little Moo" who filled our houses, and our hearts, with joy, laughter and warmth.

Zach has taken his place in heaven now. We're sure he's watching over all of us, and we're sure he helped us write this, because we needed it. Our prayers are with Cheryl and Matt, and their families.

Zachary will never be forgotten. He will live in our hearts as long as we all live.

Zachary's dad was so overcome with the loss of his son, he was unable to express his feelings. Zachary's mom, Cheryl, was able to share how he had changed their lives:

On December 29, 1995, my son Zachary Ryan Crabtree was born, but my story starts nine months earlier. The day I found out I was pregnant was a day full of joy and worry. Joy that I was pregnant and worry wondering if I would carry this child to term. My pregnancy wasn't easy. I made it through the first trimester but then things went downhill. I had morning sickness 24 hours a day, 7 days a week. I was hospitalized for dehydration and lost a total of 22 pounds during the last trimester, but I had a reason to keep going every day...a baby that gave me hope.

Just when things would begin to feel unbearable, I would get a friendly reminder from my little miracle why I needed to keep going. Finally he was born and even that wasn't easy. Four days of labor, only to have it end in a c-section. But he was here!!! A beautiful little boy named Zachary, our "Little Moo".

He was the first grandchild for both families and he was loved. In return he gave us love with every smile, every cry and every coo and life was perfect. It was perfect until one Wednesday afternoon 14 weeks later when I thought my life fell apart.

My son, my beautiful baby boy was not breathing. Every fear driven emotion I had ran through me. I had fought so hard to have this baby and now he was being ripped from my arms by a force that I had no power over. It was a long, slow process but after two days on life support he was given to God to fly with the angels. I was jealous that God had my baby and I didn't. That night and the next couple of days were the worst days of my life, but I truly believe Zachary gave me the strength I needed to take control. I knew how I wanted things to be and I knew what would make Zachary happy.

This is the point where I learned the lifelong lesson from Zachary. I was always a follower...a soft person who could be walked on, but the death of my son changed me. It wasn't a matter of it hardening me. I wasn't angry. It just showed me that I could be strong. I had an inner strength that I had never known. I was able to take charge and not fall apart. I was able to keep my life together. People around me asked if I was medicated and I laughed and replied that it was inner strength. From that point on, I was different. I did things I never thought possible, the first of which was the task of burying my child and saying a final goodbye.

We needed to have an open casket so all of our family and friends could see him for the first time and I wanted him to look perfect. I wanted the area around him to be bright and cheery so I asked for balloons instead of flowers and the place was filled with them. Zachary was a winter baby who did not know what a flower was, but he knew what a balloon was and they always made him laugh.

Zachary taught me something else...the meaning of this phrase: "Love is not a noun, it's a verb. Love must be action." It is in the action of keeping his memory alive that I am able to still show love for my son. He will always be loved and greatly missed by all who knew him but especially by his Mom and Dad. We love you, "Moo" and miss you! Play hard with all of your angel friends and keep watch over your brother and sister. They need you.

When tragedy strikes, many people are affected, and there is often a story within a story. Karen Carr, a co-worker of Cheryl's and a close friend of the Crabtree family had such a story.

I was very lucky to have known Zachary Ryan Crabtree. I worked with his Mom. She was so thrilled to find out that she was pregnant and I couldn't wait for the baby to be born. I had such great pleasure in purchasing a classic Winnie the Pooh outfit and stuffed animal as well as a tiny denim jacket. Cheryl was in labor for quite some time and Zachary was finally born via c-section. What a thrill to see the baby that had been anticipated for such a long time. He was just adorable – so tiny and absolutely BEAUTIFUL! He had me wrapped around his finger from the moment I first saw him. Over the next few months, each time I had a chance to see Zachary, the more I loved him. He would have been a lady killer when he grew up, such long eyelashes and even at one month he knew how to use them to flirt with the girls. Mom and Dad and Grandma and Grandpa Baum were so proud!

All of us at Shop'n Save who worked with Cheryl were so sad when we heard about Zachary being taken to the hospital. I immediately got the word out to the store and had everyone start praying. A card went around and I got in the car to go to [the hospital] to give my support. How could God do this? Little Zachary, so sweet, he would be all right, I just knew he would. (If it could have been willed, he WOULD be here today.)

Once I arrived at the hospital, I was welcomed by the family. Cheryl and Matt, Grandpa and Grandma Baum, Grandpa and Grandma Crabtree. Aunt Caryn, Anita...oh, I remember like it was just yesterday. I kept hoping and praying that there would be a miracle. As the family went to meet with the doctors, Aunt Caryn was asked if she wanted to go in to see Zachary and she invited me along for support. I'm so grateful for the opportunity to see Cheryl and Matt's "Little Moo" again. Aunt Caryn gave him all the reasons he should fight to stay here with us: his "firsts"...birthday, Christmas, bike ride, day of school (just to name a few.) It just wasn't to be. I was devastated. I can't even imagine what his family felt.

You know though, God had other plans for Zachary Ryan Crabtree. So many people learned so much from him. I had the opportunity to talk to a young man I knew at Zachary's calling hours that had received his drivers license back from the state of New Hampshire after losing it three years before for a DWI offense. I asked him to look around the room at the sadness and imagine if he had been driving drunk and someone's family and friends were here due to someone like him drinking and driving. To this date, this young man has not been in this kind of trouble again. I think we all learned to appreciate those that you love each and every day God chose Zachary for a reason. Ask anyone who knew him and I'm sure they could tell you how he changed their lives.

I have a unique connection of my own with little Zachary. You see, I got engaged on Christmas day the same year Zachary was born. I used to joke with Cheryl all of the time that I would have Nathan, my fiancé, deliver him since Nathan was a paramedic. When Zachary passed away, Nathan and I cried for hours. Nathan left for school in Florida in early May, just a few weeks after Zachary was gone. He was going to become a Physician's Assistant. On his way to school, he stopped in Georgia to visit his parents. On his way to the grocery store to pick up a few things for his mother at 7:00 p.m. on May 18th, Nathan Charles Thomason was killed by a drunk driver. I find peace in the fact that I know Nathan has Zachary and Zachary has Nathan in heaven. Nathan's place of burial is down in Georgia near his parents and when I need to visit him, I go to see Zachary. I'm sure that they're playing baseball, riding bikes, going swimming and doing all kinds of "guy" things together.

God works in mysterious ways. No one can change anything that has happened, but we can all remember the good times, the smiles, the wonderful baby smell, the little Moo that we all knew and loved. He will be in my heart forever. I am so fortunate to have had the opportunity to have known him and will remember him for the rest of my life. He and Nathan are my guardian angels.

Zachary died in Cheryl's arms. She told him softly it was okay to go and be with the angels. The family members that were present that day cried together as Cheryl asked for a sign that he would be okay. It was a cloudy day and a sad and dismal ride home from the hospital. Suddenly as they drove into the gray horizon on an open highway, one small piece of the sky opened up and a bright light shone through. Everyone in the car looked in amazement at the "sign" that Zachary was safe. Just then, a single clang of a bell came from nowhere. As the family wondered what was happening, it occurred to them. Much like the classic movie "It's a Wonderful Life," which told the story of when an angel gets his wings, a bell rings on earth. They knew that Zachary was in heaven and got his wings.

Life can be strange and unpredictable. Tomorrow is promised to no one. Keeping that thought at the forefront of our minds reminds us to treat everyday as though it is our last. Imagine how that one thought could change the world. Zachary's Aunt Anita summed up her feelings by saying, "The reality is that Zachary is gone. Acceptance is being able to move on. In everybody's own way, Zachary's death has been accepted and our family has moved on. Forgotten, however, is not a word in our vocabulary. You'll be in our hearts always."

When I'm faced with a challenge I don't quite understand, I think of Cheryl and how she so gracefully accepted and conquered the challenges she faced around her baby's death. When I feel sorry for myself I think of Karen Carr and the terrible ordeal she went through. When my children are pestering me for one thing or another, I hug them, knowing that tomorrow is not promised to us. I've learned many lessons from little Zachary Crabtree and I will remember him until the Good Lord takes me home to finally meet our little angel.

Mr. Music

The Story of Paul T. Giles
1911 - 1999

"Musical training is a more potent instrument than any other, because rhythm and harmony find their way into the inward places of the soul."
Plato

Dear Mr. Giles,

Yesterday I went to your house and you kindly fixed my clarinet. When I called you, you offered to fix it that very minute. I also appreciate you going out of your way and fixing it at no charge. It was very thoughtful.

On our way home, my dad made a comment that made me think. He said, "Danielle, as you grow older you'll meet many people. The people who are into their job and enjoy it will do you favors with care put into it rather than the people that don't care."

I respect your personality and I thank you for helping me when I needed it.

Your Thankful Customer,
Danielle Goodman

THE ABOVE LETTER says a lot about Paul Giles. He treated everyone who came into his life with the Golden Rule; his love of music was immeasurable; his zest for life was immense. In his home on South State Street in Concord, New Hampshire, he taught many young musicians not only about music, but about life.

I was honored to be a part of the celebration of his life. His wife, Priscilla, called the funeral home on the morning of his death and asked for Mr. Bennett. Mr. Bennett, my mentor and former owner of the Home, had retired several years earlier. Priscilla insisted on meeting with Mr. Bennett and was somewhat uncomfortable talking with anyone else. Mr. Bennett and Mr. Giles had known one another for years, and their relationship offered the comfort level Priscilla wanted. I knew Mr. Bennett would not be able to fill her needs, so I made it my mission to do whatever I had to do for Priscilla to be comfortable.

Mr. Giles was a well-known, much loved member of the community. As a result, his funeral was big and there were a multitude of details to handle. He'd been a member and director of a local band, and his son was a member of the Fire Department's Color Guard. I took over 100 phone calls that week answering questions about the funeral. It was obviously going to be a high profile service and I couldn't afford mistakes.

I sat with the Giles family to plan the service and, less than five minutes after they'd left, I got a phone call from our local newspaper, the *Concord Monitor*. The article ran is as follows:

Teacher known to many as "Mr. Music" dead at 87
Paul Giles gave lessons, fixed instruments and
played clarinet in the Nevers' Band for 48 years.
By Amy McConnell, *Concord Monitor* staff

When local music lovers gather on balmy summer nights to listen to the Nevers' Band, they will no longer hear the sound of Paul Giles's clarinet.

Giles, 87, died Friday night at Concord Hospital. A devoted musician whom some people called "Concord's Mr. Music," Giles gave local children music lessons for nearly five decades, played clarinet in the Nevers' Band for 48 years and conducted the band for 26 years, until 1985.

Her husband lived a wonderful life, according to Priscilla Giles, who has played percussion to Giles's woodwind for most of their years together.

"He did, and it was all musical," she said.

A native of Haverhill, Mass., Giles took the train into Boston after class at Haverhill High School to study with Augusto Vinnini and Francis Findley at the New England Conservatory of Music. He later attended the National Orchestra and Band Camp in Michigan and the Curtis Institute of Music in Philadelphia.

After graduation, Giles taught orchestra conducting and music education as an associate professor at the University of New Hampshire, according to his wife. They married in 1950 and moved to the Concord area, where Giles taught music in public schools in Concord, Penacook, Tilton and Northwood, as well as at Bishop Brady High School.

Giles was the director of instrumental music at St. Paul's School until his retirement about 20 years ago. Even after retirement, Priscilla Giles said, he continued giving lessons at St. Paul's on a part-time basis until just a few years ago.

In Concord, Giles's decades of teaching, his inexpensive, while-you-wait instrument repair business, and the many thousands of lessons he gave made him a well-known and well-loved figure, according to his daughter, Deborah Giles Lincoln.

Everybody in town who knew her father sat and looked out the window of what he called his "torture chamber" – the fabulously cluttered room where he repaired instruments and gave woodwind lessons, she said.

And when her father went out in public, former students always remembered him, even after years had passed since their last lesson, said Lincoln, who sat in the "student chair" beside her father's old seat as she talked. All around her lay sheets of music, clarinet mouthpieces, tiny drill bits, screwdrivers, pliers, and tools her father had made when a store-bought tool wouldn't work.

"He could not go out and eat at a restaurant [when] someone would stop and say, 'Hello Mr. Giles. You taught me the clarinet in high school,'" Lincoln said.

At his peak, Giles gave 45 lessons per week to area children, who would line the hallway of his home on South State Street after school, at night and on weekends. The constant sound of students of all ages practicing their lessons became the heartbeat of the household, according to Giles's children, who remember listening to the sound of music as they drifted off to sleep.

"It seemed like there was something wrong when you didn't hear it, said his son, Doug Giles.

Giles stopped giving lessons only last June, when he began feeling unwell, his wife said. For 2 years, a defibrillator and pacemaker had allowed her husband to give music lessons, play summer concerts with the Nevers' Band and perform at local events like parades and First Night celebrations, Priscilla Giles said.

When a doctor examined her husband nearly three years ago, he said Giles's constant activity made it possible to use a pacemaker, according to Priscilla Giles.

"The doctor told him at the time he'd never put one in a man that old," she said. "He said, 'We don't put them in couch potatoes and you're not a couch potato.'"

Priscilla Giles said she is hoping part of the Nevers' Band will play at her husband's memorial service, scheduled for next Sunday at South Congregational Church. She doesn't yet know whether she will continue playing with the group without her husband.

"I can't think about next year yet," she said.

(Reprinted with permission from the Concord Monitor)

There always seems to be plenty to say or write about someone after they die. In 1996, however, when Mr. Giles was still alive and active at 84 years old, Andy Hamilton wrote an essay about him for a Concord High School Class entitled "Important Person in My Life".

I'm sure you've seen him, maybe you've even met him. Go to any high school, junior high school or elementary school music concert and there he is, front row, with a wide smile on his face. Even if you've never seen him, he is a friend.

I met Mr. Giles three years ago, and ever since, whenever someone mentions his name, I smile. Technically, he is my clarinet instructor, but he teaches as much about life as he does the clarinet.

Mr. Giles has lived many years and seen many things. His white hair is a testimony to that. His bright eyes twinkle with the gleam of a child and the glimmer of a smile is always on his round, aging face. His Yankee accent and grandfather-like aura complete his appearance.

It is said that you can tell a lot about a man by his hands and this is no exception. Mr. Giles' hands are a perfect fit for all the instruments he plays. They are big and would seem clumsy until you see him fix a broken clarinet. He takes apart the instrument and puts it back together, with all the tiny screws and minuscule springs. I believe if it makes music he can fix it and play it.

What sets Mr. Giles apart from everyone else is not just his amazing musical talent but it is how he cares about people. He comes from a simpler time, when people were nicer and cared more, and he has not lost that concept. Whenever I see him on the street or in a store he always greets me with a smile and something interesting to say.

Another thing that I love about Mr. Giles is the funny anecdotes he is always telling me. From the time he got an ivory ring for the end of an old, wooden clarinet, to the time he met the man who saved the Prince of England's life. One of my favorite stories is the one about when Mr. Giles music teacher told him not to come back for lessons until Mr. Giles had memorized all the scales. Well, he worked for a week and came back to the music teacher. The music teacher was surprised to see Mr. Giles come back so soon, but he was even more surprised to hear him play all the scales perfectly. It seems to me that all of Mr. Giles' stories carry an important message about life. The moral of the story may not always pop out at you but it is there, waiting for someone to realize what he is saying. Another story of Mr. Giles I like is when he played under the direction of John Philip Sousa. It boggles my mind to think of all the wonderful and amazing things he has done.

I would not paint an accurate picture of Mr. Giles if I did not include a paragraph about his special, improvised gadgets. One of my favorite do-hickeys is one that he uses to see if the pads on the instrument fit correctly. It is composed of a small light bulb affixed to an electrical wire that he plugs into the outlet. This contraption slithers down the throat of the instrument like some beast swallowing spaghetti. He also has a small handmade blowtorch, a pump organ hooked up to a vacuum cleaner engine, and other...interesting tools.

Thursday night, at 5:00, is a special time for me because this is when I meet with Mr. Giles. We spend as much time talking as we do playing. We have jam sessions, we talk about each piece of music, he tells me what is interesting in the news, and he tweaks and tests my clarinet.

I know I am missing a lot but Mr. Giles is such a colorful character that no piece of writing can do him justice. So, I guess I'll finish by thanking Mr. Giles for all the help he has given me...but most of all...for brightening up my life and for being a friend.

That's quite a testament to the man's character. It seems he made an impression on many people. Jane and Charles Lemeland wrote to Priscilla in a sympathy card:

"Paul was more than special. I think you'll remember, Priscilla, my saying years ago when Lise was in fourth or fifth grade that I would bring Lise to him even if he didn't teach the flute. The way he interacted with children was an inspiration...so loving and humorous. And what he taught was more than music...life."

Even Mr. Giles' facial expressions made people feel good, as Alice Davis wrote:

"Houston and I are deeply saddened by the news of Paul. We never saw him without a big smile on his face and joy in his heart. He gave so much to our community and truly lived life to its fullest – a wonderful role model on how to do it right!"

One of the greatest things you could do for anyone is to change their life in a positive way. Here are excerpts of how Mr. Giles changed Emily Elliot's life, as told by her mother:

...Emily began clarinet lessons with Mr. Giles when she was in the seventh grade...She is now a junior at Concord High School.

Emily loves music. She found a kindred spirit in Mr. Giles. They loved sharing music stories, and she was thrilled when he played duets with her during lessons.

Last year was a difficult year for Emily. She was very ill for a long period of time and often had difficulty playing the music she so loved. Every lesson day she looked for the "waving hand in the window" when she arrived at the house. I could see her relax immediately. When her hands would shake and not allow her to play, or medication made her so sleepy she could barely focus, Mr. Giles simply told her it was ok, and they would just talk for awhile. He could always make her smile, and she always felt comfortable. Music lessons were a time for acceptance and a break from the otherwise very difficult days. During this time he often shared his own medical stories with her as well, and she would end her lessons reminding him to rest and take care of himself.

She misses him greatly. But, she is still playing, and intends to audition for All State this year for the first time. She told Mr. Giles when she was a freshman that she was too afraid to audition, that she would "mess up." Last year she was not well enough to consider taking on the All State Auditions. I remember him telling her that it's ok to make mistakes, to take a deep breath and give it all you've got. "If you're going to make a mistake, make it a good one!" he laughingly told her.

...We were blessed to have known him. He gave Emily a wonderful gift – to believe in herself.

He even made the people he worked with feel good when they otherwise may not have. From Holly Tepe, a former co-worker at St. Paul's School:

"I was very sorry to hear of Paul's death. He was a really special man and the light of my life in the music department. If I came to school in a bad mood, his smile and a funny story or joke would cheer me up in a moment. It was impossible not to smile back when he smiled at me!"

Mr. Giles' passion for music, and his pure talent in passing it on to his students, was unsurpassed. Here's what two of his students wrote to Mrs. Giles shortly after Paul's passing.

From former student Annette (Lawrence) Backus:

"...He was a wonderful man who made a huge difference in my life. I had started viola lessons in fourth grade – and hated them. In the sixth grade I started clarinet with Paul. His wonderful temperament and teaching style, along with an obvious love of kids and music, made me a convert. I played clarinet through college, and have continued off and on as my schedule permits. What a legacy!"

From former student Kathleen (Wells) McDonald:

"...I will always be grateful for the care and concern that he demonstrated in every one of my oboe lessons. He always made me feel good about myself, and he brought out the best I had. While I had always dreaded my piano lessons (despite a very good teacher), I loved my oboe lessons...I hope he enjoyed the satisfaction of knowing he had given so many of us a lifelong gift – the appreciation of music that one can only have from being able to play a musical instrument."

Other students at Saint Paul's School (SPS) paid tribute to Mr. Giles memory in the Winter 1999 edition of "Millville Memories". The tributes spoke of Mr. Giles' love of music and his unique ability to share that joy with his students (reprinted with permission from St. Paul's School):

From Meg (Ziegler) Ferguson '77 and Harry Ferguson '77:

"My husband and I met in the SPS band and have enjoyed keeping in touch with Mr. Giles since leaving SPS. Our two children were fortunate to see Paul and Priscilla several times. We remember our daughter sitting in his lap at around age two, blowing a penny whistle while Paul did the fingering so they played a tune together.

That was Paul Giles at his best: showing children of all ages that they could, and should, play music for the sheer joy of it. We remember him telling clarinet players to raise their eyebrows so they would hit high notes; making unbelievably gruesome faces during rehearsals, changing frustration (or lassitude) into laughter; telling a hapless snare drummer to make it sound like a mosquito biting a tin can; smushing a bug on a piece of sheet music and drawing a tombstone and "R.I.P" around the spot; and telling a timid trombone player to 'play it again, and this time REALLY LET ME HAVE IT!' with his fist flying through the air. He never hesitated to tell us that it took more muscles to make a frown than to make a smile.

When Mr. Giles retired in 1977, the Giles Band Prize was created in his honor by the Band of 1977, his family and many friends. There is a nice plaque in the Music Building. Mr. Giles was an important teacher and mentor for many SPS students for many, many years."

David Rea '67 wrote:

"I remember joining the SPS Band in Third Form. My dad had told me, 'If you miss out on the opportunity to play for a man like Paul Giles, you'll regret it for the rest of your life.' Four years later, after practice sessions that were hilarious, concerts that were thrilling, brass ensembles atop the Chapel tower, and trips to NYC to play in Madison Square Garden that had me awe-struck, I realized that, as usual, parents are always right. Mr. Giles was an energetic conductor and a consummate showman with a great sense of humor. But, I think what has stuck with me is that he truly loved music and he had a passion for teaching music to young people...even those, like me, who had very marginal talent."

Doug Giles said of his father:

"I remember hearing someone say that as a young man they were dismayed at how little their father knew but by the time that person had grown up and built a family of his own he was pleased at how much his father had learned. Well, eventually I figured out what he meant.

It took me a long time to realize what a wonderful role model my father was. In a culture whose values seem so elusive he was a jewel of faith and passion. He looked at each new day as an opportunity. His morning thoughts were of what he could do, not what he had to do. His mind never stopped, always looking and exploring and he instilled in me a belief that all you needed was an oil can and a screw driver and you could fix almost anything. A little oil to smooth things out and something to pry with so you could see what was inside. He wasn't perfect but he taught me to look at the possibilities.

His life was about possibilities and yet I can't imagine there was something that wasn't in it. It will take a lifetime to learn all he had to offer...and I am looking forward to it."

The eulogy was delivered by his daughter, Debbie Giles Lincoln.

...I would like to warn you that while I'm up here, I will at some point start crying. I hope this doesn't offend you because as you might imagine, I seem to have no control over it. So when I do cry, sit back, relax and join in!

Not only have I inherited the Giles 'gift of gab' but I have also inherited a lifetime of stories, experiences and insight. It's difficult to condense my 47 years with Dad into a few paragraphs. Those of you who know Dad and me, realize that we have always had a special kind of relationship.

Last Friday night, as we were all taking turns holding Dad's hand, in the hospital, I tried not to think about how much a part of my life those hands have been and how much I was going to miss them.

Those hands have always been there for me. They helped me build my first paper-mache map of New Hampshire. They helped me get an 'A' on my Junior High science project about solar cells...Those hands of his built the coolest tree house for us in the old apple tree in the back yard. His hands refurbished and personalized hand-me-down bicycles so they'd be special and look brand new. He was always customizing our toys, furniture and in later years our households. He truly was the original "Yankee Mr. Fix-it." He repaired alarm clocks, hair dryers, smoothed over spoons that had been through the garbage disposal, and soldered my mother's favorite kitchen knife over and over again. He pounded out the dent I put in the rear fender of their white station wagon after I had backed into the fire hydrant.

And...what Dad couldn't fix – he'd oil. But we all knew Dad had "gone over the edge of "Mr. Fix-it-ness" when he took his dremel tool and smoothed over the sharp edge of Mom's broken tooth.

Family gatherings, especially Christmas, really brought out the kid in Dad...even more so than usual. It wasn't Christmas until Grampa Paul had hidden in the closet and barked like a dog, totally confusing all the grandchildren. His magical hands had quite a repertoire of tricks right down from the fake hypodermic needle, to the hammer that sounded like breaking glass, to the windup woodpecker that drilled a hole into his forehead. And boy do I remember those hands of his reaching into his jacket pocket to retrieve a joke he needed to share with everyone.

Our family pets were always a big part of Dad's life...Dad was the "Dr. Dolittle" of the dog world and spent some of his most precious moments with the loving companionship of the family dogs. Those hands of his knew the right time to nuzzle and the exact spot to scratch. (On the dog, that is...)

Dad loved nature. His hands introduced me to the Northern Lights. They pointed out the clumps of Lady Slippers he loved. Those hands often carried many a bug into the house so we could analyze the interesting pattern on its wings or see how it camouflaged itself. He'd drag us out at night to watch the bats gobble up mosquitoes or watch the crawfish at camp hide from the beam of our flashlights. And believe it or not we spent endless evening hours "hypnotizing frogs."

I think everyone in the family will agree that Dad's largest, yet fondest, undertaking was the building of the camp in Loudon. In 1958 Mom and Dad bought a heavily wooded piece of land on the side of a steep hill at Clough's Pond. Dad's industrious hands cleared the land and built a small bunk house to house four people...COZILY. Four years later, he built the log cabin that remained his pride and joy. Whenever showing folks around, he'd step back with his arms folded across his chest and gloat, "Not bad for a musician, eh?"

Then, those hands that I've come to love so much led me out into the world of music. Dad was savvy enough to make sure my first few performances were successful by my playing duets with him. That way <u>he</u> could cover up any mistakes I'd make and he could warm up the audience by having them clap for me <u>before</u> I had played anything!

And we all know how Dad's fingers played the clarinet! Those huge but nimble fingers jumped over the keys as he played at a particular faculty recital in St. Paul's School Chapel. Mozart's Clarinet Concerto. I wore a quaint velvet dress and was seated to Dad's right as he performed. You see, this was my big debut as a page turner. I fervently counted measures, carefully turned the page, then watched Dad's hands gently reach over during a rest to turn the page BACK. It seems I had turned the page, 64 measures TOO SOON!

While teaching at St. Paul's, Dad had the good fortune to meet many musical 'greats' who were invited to the school for lectures and concerts. Musicians such as Dave Brubeck, Joe Morello and Aaron Copland. I don't know of another person alive who in the company of such musical magnates, would take the spoons off the dining table and use them to play 'Mary Had a Little Lamb' on his head for them!

Since my page turning debut, most of you probably know that I have gone on to follow in dad's footsteps in music education. When I secured my first teaching job...I asked Dad for any advice or words of wisdom. 'Yup,' he said, 'Get in good with the custodians and the ladies in the cafeteria." Dad would never ask the custodians to do anything he wasn't prepared to help with. It was his unpretentious manner that endeared him to both his students and his co-workers.

Mom and Dad have been my biggest fans and cheerleaders throughout my teaching career. I think they have attended EVERY concert my school kids have ever performed. It has always amazed me how two people can hear every conceivable version of 'Hot Cross Buns' and still keep coming back for more. As the holiday concert season approaches, I'll desperately miss Dad's hands as they tape record each one of those elementary musical extravaganzas for a post concert 'Hot Cross Buns' critique.

Today I haven't told you much about the public Paul Giles, the band director, the teacher, the professional. But you know all about that part. I've been sharing the funny stories that seemed to punctuate his life...the stories that I will derive comfort from in the coming days. Through Dad's intense love for life, learning and sharing, I've learned that life is indeed, 'too important to be taken seriously.'

Before I sit down and finally stop talking, I'd like to publicly thank Mom for devoting her every moment to Dad in his recent illness and for keeping him safe and in the shelter of the camp and family he loved so much. I'd also like to thank Dad. The only reason I can stand up here and share this with all of you is because his hands that I've come to love so much, are still holding me up.

What an amazing man! He took the gifts God gave him and used them to bless everyone he met. What struck me most was his humanity. It would have been very easy for him to shelter himself from "regular people." But in his mind, he too was a "regular person." He and Priscilla shared a wonderful life together and they enriched my life through their example. Priscilla will carry on with the memory of Paul in her heart every day. When I see her at the grocery store or the gas station, she has a smile and a hug for me and, of course, a story about Paul. His memory and legacy will endure forever. It is fitting to recall the words delivered by Rev. Dr. Philip Randall Giles, his brother, at Mr. Giles memorial service:

"Life has given more than death can take away, let us then be glad he lived and loved life among us."

If They Could See Me Now

The Story of Sue V. Bickford
1931 - 1999

*"Man, unlike the animal, has never learned that
the sole purpose of life is to enjoy it."*
Samuel Butler

HOW MANY PEOPLE fall in love with their tax collector? In the town of Epsom, New Hampshire, everyone. So much so, they elected her as one of their three Selectman. She loved everybody and they loved her. That was the nature of Sue Bickford.

She was a hard working woman who raised three children: Bill, Paula and Joni. She also ran a successful business with her husband: Bickford's Sport Center. Sam and Sue eventually transferred the business to their children and Sue decided to devote her time to her family and to making the town of Epsom a better place.

After Sue's passing, Tony Soltani, himself a public servant in Epsom, wrote the following letter to the local newspaper:

Last week Epsom lost a great friend and an old advocate. Sue Bickford, who had virtually served in every capacity within the town government, died of a sudden illness to the surprise and dismay of many townspeople. Sue was a great public servant who always gave her time without asking for anything in return. She always explained her mission and function as looking out for the people of Epsom. During her career as a public servant, Sue saved the town well in excess of $1,000,000.00. She was a community leader and a role model to many members of the generation that followed hers. On a personal level, she was a good friend and a reliable confidant whom I will dearly miss. If I am able to do a fraction of what Sue did for the people of Epsom, I should be satisfied. Sue will be greatly missed, but never forgotten.

As a 40-year town resident, Sue held positions as tax collector, Selectman and, at the time of her death, was a member of the town budget committee. Her greatest gift to the town however, was as a tireless volunteer...a trait that endeared her to many of the townspeople.

She also seemed to be happy and to know how to enjoy life. A friend of hers, Gail Gagnon, wrote this in a card to the family:

"Words cannot express the overwhelming feeling of losing such a wonderful person. Sue will be missed at the shop. She always had a smile and a 'Good morning girls!' when she came in, and a 'Have a nice weekend!' when she left. She always said she loved her children and grandchildren and that they were her life."

Besides politics and her volunteering, she participated in several performances of the "Friends of Epsom Shows." Three months after her passing, the Friends dedicated a portion of the program to her:

In Memoriam – Sue Bickford
August 24, 1931 – July 3, 1999

Saddened by the loss of their fellow thespian, the Friends of Epsom Shows dedicate their 1999 performances to the memory of Sue Bickford.

We shall long remember the Ethel Mermanish-gravelly voice of Sue's rendition of *Won't You Come Home Bill Bailey.*

You each have your own fond memory of Sue's many stage characters...maybe her duet with Carroll Stevens, or her being serenaded with *Hello Susie...*or maybe Snow White with the seven dwarfs...*Sister Kate...Gimme a Little Kiss*, or, most fittingly, *If They Could See Me Now!*

She was truly one of a kind and she has left us all with precious memories.

Precious memories indeed. Whether it was her famous Italian dishes, winning Bingo games, or spending special days with her grandchildren, she left precious memories for everyone who knew her.

Once, the young men gathering at her home were bragging about who was the best at "shotguns" (a "shotgun" is a beer drinking game where you punch a hole in the bottom of a beer can so when you crack the top open, you have no choice but to guzzle it all in one gulp because of the pressure created by the hole in the bottom. Last one standing, wins.) Sue decided to challenge the champion, who just happened to be her son, Bill. And she won!

Sue was also adept at games of chance. One night, her daughter Joni and Joni's fiancé, Richard, joined her at Bingo. Before the game, they purchased "pull" tickets, which offer a chance to win $250 by picking a lucky number and color. As Richard was on his way to pick a color, Sue called to him, "YELLOW!" But Richard preferred orange. He realized he should have listened to her when yellow was the color that was pulled.

She was also full of surprises. When her children were 16, 14 and 10, she planned a trip to Disney World as a surprise for son Bill, the 10 year old. The girls packed his clothes without him knowing and all the kids went to the airport thinking they were going to send their parents off. When they arrived, Sue and her husband asked the kids if they wanted to see the inside of the plane and they all boarded. When the flight attendant told them to sit down and buckle up, Bill began to panic since he was still on the plane. That was when Sue asked him if he'd like to go to Disney World!

Her family describes Sue as the most giving person in the world. Sue's daughter-in-law and two sons-in-law were just as much her children as were her own. On the day after Christmas, she started preparing for the next Christmas. In fact, although she died in July, there were gifts under the tree for everyone the following December 25th. She knit detailed, personalized sweaters, mittens and socks specially designed for each child and grandchild. Christmas day was her favorite and she would put on a spread fit for a king. People would come and go on Christmas

Eve and into the night on Christmas Day. And no one left empty handed.

Sue's story brings back wonderful memories of times I had with my Grandfather. Not a day goes by when I don't wish I could spend five minutes with him. Sometimes though, I get what I believe to be a sign that he is still with me. Sue's daughter-in-law, Denise, had a similar experience:

"Three months before Nana died, I lost my father to cancer. He was the male version of Nana; lovable, huggable and full of kisses. She helped me so much to make it through the most difficult time of my life. Suddenly she was gone. I thought my world just came to an end. First my wonderful Dad, and now my mentor, my confidante, my beautiful mother-in-law. How could life get any worse?

A few months later, my birthday came. Birthdays will never be the same without Nana around. She made everyone's birthday special. I told my husband I wasn't in a festive mood and although he was wonderful to me, I simply couldn't get happy. I went to bed thankful that this dreary day without my Dad and my Mother-in-law was over.

That night in a dream, Nana was cooking for us (like she always did) and Dad was an angel. I entered Nana and Papa's house and asked Nana if she needed help. She declined my offer so I went into the living room where Dad (the angel) was sitting in Nana's chair. As I was telling my Dad how much I loved him, Nana yelled from the kitchen, 'Who are you talking to?' I said, 'Dad.' She then came around the corner happily surprised and said 'Oh my god, it is your Dad!'

That was a sign to me that Nana and Dad would always be there for me and were watching over all of us."

Whether it was Sue's volunteering, Mrs. Bickford's political prowess, Mom's knitted sweaters, the gravelly-voiced thespian, or Nana's famous Italian cooking, Sue Bickford touched many lives.

Her example has taught me to live life to it's fullest. It taught me to smile more often, because a pleasant smile brings a good feeling to everyone around you. It taught me to stay involved with my community, as someone out there could benefit from what I have to offer. It taught me to always have something set aside as a surprise for my children and grandchildren, as it just might "make their life." Most of all, Sue Bickford's example taught me the true meaning of joy. Spreading joy, receiving joy, and sharing joy. With all the joy there is in heaven, Sue must be thinking, "If they could see me now".

An Empty House, An Empty Heart

The Story of Celestine Humphreys
1912 - 1999

"There is only one happiness in life, to love and be loved."
George Sand

CELESTINE HUMPHREYS HAS been described by family and friends as a saint. She was married to Arthur Humphreys for 62 years and they raised three children: Arthur Jr., Celestine (Sis), and Paul.

As the children were growing up, Arthur loved his family and wanted the best for them, including — in his tough New York way — disciplining his children. As any child will tell you things aren't always fair, and that's when Celestine would smooth things over.

With the family grown and more grandchildren arriving every year, Arthur finally retired. When Celestine's health began to fail, the Humphreys decided to move from Long Island to Concord, N. H. to be near their youngest, Paul.

Arthur dedicated himself to taking care of "his little Angel". Their love and devotion to one another was unquestionable. Sometimes, Arthur would kiss Celestine on the cheek, one right after another, until she would have to tell him to go away!

One morning, Arthur went to the kitchen to make coffee. He took it back to the bedroom to wake Celestine and when he touched her, she was cold. He begged her to wake up, but he knew she was gone.

I arrived at their little white house at 8:00 a.m. The minute I walked in, I was greeted by a cute little 89-year-old man, slightly hunched over and 90% blind, but otherwise in good shape. He reenacted what had happened earlier with tears streaming down his face, saying "I lost my baby, my love, my little angel. She's cold, she's cold." I put my arms around him and tried to comfort him as best as I could, reassuring him we would take good care of her. He wanted to spend a few more minutes with her before we took her to the Funeral Home and, ever the gentleman, he poured me a cup of coffee to drink while I waited for him. When it was time to go, he thanked me for my help, hugged me, kissed me on the cheek, and blew kisses to his wife as the hearse pulled away.

During the viewing at the funeral home, Arthur never left the casket. He frequently leaned over to kiss her on the lips, so much so that he smeared her lipstick and his daughter had to ask me to fix it! Before the casket was closed, Arthur asked that two hundred dollars in cash be placed in the casket with her. He said, "It's the last money she counted. It was in her pocketbook and I want it to be with her forever."

Over two years have passed since Celestine died. Their house is exactly the way it was the day she died. Her side of the bed is covered in plastic so as not to disturb the blanket or pillow where she last laid her head. Stuffed teddy bears surround the bed to keep an eye on her side as "security guards" and pictures of her are everywhere. Her clothes are still in the closet with the last dress she wore specially marked and placed.

That's an awful lot of love and a very broken heart. Arthur is coping as best he can. He wrote Celestine a letter a year after she died. It sits framed in their bedroom. It says this:

Dear Celestine Ann Humphreys,

My dear sweet Cel I love you very much. You'll always be my sweetheart. I have a very aching heart and nobody can take your place. I love you more than I do my life. You're the sweetheart of my life. I'll always miss you. My little rosebud and my hummingbird tongue. My little daffodil. You are sweeter than sweet. All your children love you. I miss your cooking. It's hard to have a cup of coffee without you. I miss giving you your tea.

Half of my life is gone without you. The other half is for my son.
Paul misses you very much, too. I'm living a tough life without you.
Always loving you and missing you very very much.

Your sweetheart husband,
Arthur

Kenny Rogers sang a song that describes this very situation to a tee. It's titled, "Love Don't Live Here Anymore."

Love Don't Live Here Anymore
Eric Kaz/Linda Thompson 1999
Warner Tamerlame Publishing Corp./
Brandon Brody Music

This is the house that love built
Memories of you built in each wall
Warm tender scenes, still haunt my dreams
Thought I just heard your voice in the hall
Mirrors reflect all the heartache I feel
Smiling photographs don't seem real
Chorus: Nothings been moved, but everything's changed
Each chair is in place just my life's rearranged
The wind cries your name through each window and door
Love don't live here...Love don't live here anymore
The firelight still glows a pale blue
Mantle is cool holding pictures of you
Your scent lingers there, in the bed that we share
The last plant I sent is in bloom
These rooms are unkind to play tricks on my mind
I can't see how you'd leave without me
Chorus: Nothings been moved, but everything's changed
Each chair is in place just my life's rearranged
The wind cries your name through each window and door
Love don't live here...Love don't live here anymore

There are many reasons Arthur loved and adored Celestine. Most of them are small: life is full of simple pleasures and they shared many of them in their 62 years together. Celestine always put Arthur first. When she went shopping for any occasion, she always got something for Arthur before she got what she went for

41

in the first place. Her love for him was so strong, when her health began to fail she told Arthur she hoped they would die together. Morning, noon and night they were consumed with each other. Those who knew them could see the love and devotion they shared. No wonder Arthur describes Celestine as "the perfect wife."

Celestine wasn't famous or even well known in town. The difference she made was with her husband and children. She knew when all was said and done, what she really had was her family. In particular, she had her husband – kids grow up and start families of their own. Her partner in life was God's gift to her and she treasured that gift until her dying breath.

Arthur treasured her as well and continues to treasure her memory. He has vowed to keep her memory alive by showing everyone the importance of loving their spouse. He knows all too well that tomorrow may be the last day any of us see our husbands or wives again.

The world is filled with temptation, infidelity and selfishness and Celestine was a model of love, grace and selfless service to her husband and lifetime partner. Arthur returned all she gave. It may take me years to reach that level of commitment, but with each day I see my wife is the one constant in my life and, when all is said and done, all I'll really have is her. Thank you, Mrs. Humphreys, for showing me the true meaning of love and marriage.

A Family Man's Legacy

The Story of Paul Finnegan
1950 - 1999

"The family is one of nature's masterpieces."
George Santayana

IT WAS A beautiful sunny Sunday in September and my partner, Terry Jelley, and I had just finished doing the house chores in the Funeral Home when we received a "call." We were to go to a house in Pembroke, N.H. to get Paul Finnegan, who had died peacefully at home after a grueling battle with cancer.

When we arrived at the house, we waited outside for half an hour while the family spent more time with Paul. While waiting, we stretched our legs and noticed an old overweight beagle peeking around the corner. As I approached the dog to pat her, she meekly turned away and waddled off. Each time the dog got close to us, I tried to approach her; and each time, she would waddle away in fear.

When we finally entered the house and began moving Paul onto our stretcher, the dog stood there watching, looking like her heart was breaking. If the family pet was this upset, you can imagine the pain of Paul's wife, Sheila and their two young sons, Brendan, 16 and Daniel, 11.

What stood out the most to me about Paul Finnegan was the fact that he was a true family man. His wife and sons placed particularly touching messages on our "Memory Angels" at Paul's Memorial Service.

Sheila wrote:

"Paul, As you know angels are very special to me and after your last words, writing a note to you on an angel means even more. My thoughts are with you at least a hundred times a day but I get through each struggle with a lot of tears and a lot of love. You would be as proud of the boys as I have been. They are handling themselves with incredible grace and strength, as was the example you set. We have continued all our normal activities. All of the love that surrounds us helps to take away some of the sadness and anger. I'm striving to be what you would have wanted. Sometimes it's easy, sometimes it's hard. But we are ok and will continue to be ok. I derive some comfort in knowing you are in a peaceful place. Know that you live in our hearts."

Brendan wrote:

"Dear Dad, I miss you. I hope you are in a good and better place. Well, I know that you are. We are doing good as a family. We have bonded together and we are getting through it. Thanks for all the good times."

Daniel wrote:

"Dad, I miss you. How is it up there? Things are going fine down here. I broke my thumb. You wouldn't believe how much your help in basketball has made a difference in my playing. I made Mr. Paris's team and I'm one of the best defenders. I did real good on my report card. I think I made High Honors or Honors. The pictures of you mean a lot to me. I miss you very much.

Making a difference in our own world is really what counts in life. Obviously Paul made a difference with his family. He also made a difference in the lives of his friends. Debbie Babson, the wife of Sheila's cousin, wrote the following letter to Paul who, unfortunately, died before he had a chance to read it.

I want you to know how much we've enjoyed being a part of you and Sheila's lives. We've had a lot of good times together over the years, whether we were at Cedar Pond, Concord, or at Gurnet Point. You are one of the nicest men we've ever met and have all the qualities we hope our son will have as a man. You are what every mother and father hope their son will be.

You are a wonderful husband, an awesome Dad and an unbelievable friend. I learned this when I saw how many people supported the Lourdes trip. It was hard to believe one person could have such a huge support system.

We want you to know that we love you, we'll always be there for Sheila and the kids and that we'll never, ever forget you.

From now until the end of our time we'll never float the creek again without first thinking of you. Thanks for letting us be a part of your life.

Paul's Funeral Mass took place at Immaculate Heart of Mary Catholic Church in Concord, N.H. As the pallbearers carried the casket into the church, a bagpiper played "Danny Boy." The service was wonderful, just as Paul would have wanted. The most powerful and telling part of the Mass was when Sheila gave his Eulogy entitled, "Farewell to Paul."

First, let me begin by reassuring you all that I haven't lost my sense of humor. After more than 20 years with me, with my high energy and task oriented nature, this man is finally getting a rest.

I want to tell you about part of our journey, which has been a learning experience and growth catalyst, albeit painful for our family, as well as for many of you who have shared it with us along the way.

Paul was the perfect candidate for melanoma, with his fair skin and a love of the outdoors that extended from his childhood at Cedar Pond, through his running, hiking, canoeing and skiing. He called himself a melanoma "Poster Child." The truth is that all the MRI's and catscans that detected the growth of tumors that destroyed his body, never saw into the true nature of his gentle soul. His enduring patience and easy going, accepting personality couldn't be seen on a slide. All the toxins that were flushed through his body in hopes of killing the cancer, never once poisoned his determination, his will to live, nor his strong faith. He tolerated the intensive treatments as a lighthouse withstands a storm, looming straight and tall, shining like a beacon of light, helping those in distress or blinded by fog to find their way. His attitude astounded all who came in contact with him, including myself. His openness to talk about his disease made others feel comfortable. Yes, Paul became discouraged about his fate and fearful of his destiny, but continued to battle the cancer with grace, dignity and admirable courage.

One night, after we learned of the invasion into the liver, I had a vivid and scary dream. There was a rock wall with earth above. Rocks were falling from the wall, leaving gaping holes in the foundation. I tried frantically to put the wall back together but to no avail. I awoke in tears and filled with anxiety. It did not take an MSW to see the symbolism. Paul has been my foundation for over 20 years, longer than I knew my own mother. He has been my security, my best friend, my lover and confidant. He knew all my unpleasant sides and it did not squelch his love for me. There will be a huge emptiness in our lives. My children are too young to lose their father, but he has given them a solid foundation and more attention than many receive in a lifetime. From that we may derive some comfort, hope and gratitude. Any fatherly advice he never had a chance to give them as they matured, can be derived from his example.

Even from his boyhood, when Paul made a commitment, it was there. He wasn't just a boy scout, he became an eagle scout at 16. He didn't just ski, he raced on the ski team for Berlin High and at UNH and later joined the ski patrol at Wildcat. He didn't just run, he trained and ran 6 marathons, not an easy task for a man of his size. He wasn't just a social worker, he became a board member and President of NH NASW and later served on a national committee, a total of an 8 year commitment. Social work values were at the core of his career. He gave up work on his dissertation for his doctorate only because of failing health but completed 8 years of course work toward his Ph.D. in social work. His commitment to his family was unwavering as he coached his boys in basketball, soccer and little league, season after season, shared with them his treasured Cedar Pond and taught them to ski. I never once questioned his loyalty to me. Paul rarely had to apologize for his treatment of people, which was always fair, direct and gentle. I will miss most, his ability to analyze a situation and think through a response or solution which was not reactive or emotional. It was a gift I have never encountered the likes of in anyone else. I pray that I have learned enough from him to continue this process.

Paul gave up a lot this past year but the only thing that mattered to him was things he will miss with his children. Through this journey, Paul's faith in God grew stronger and deeper. I truly believe that angels took him.

Not too long ago, a friend said to us, "Where there is great love, miracles happen." It is true, we did not have the physical miracle we were hoping for. The miracle was seen by anyone who entered our home the last day of Paul's life and saw the way family and friends pulled it together to provide the most natural and beautiful experience of death. It was actually wonderful to see two children care so lovingly for their dying father. The gift and miracle of the Holy Spirit was bestowed on us in the form of the love and caring we have received from our circle of family and friends throughout this experience. Many of you have shared this journey with Paul, Brendan, Dan and myself. You have become part of our lives and family, sharing day to day burdens. The support we have received from the members of this church and community has lifted our hearts and lightened our heavy load immeasurably. Our trip to Lourdes was a wonderful and unforgettable experience which we will treasure forever. For all of it, Paul, myself and the boys thank you from the bottom of our hearts. For my children, this painful experience has been so colored with love and prayer, that I am eternally grateful.

So farewell, dearest Paul. As Simon Birch said, "Enter eternity. Let the angels guide you."

During communion, Van Morrison's "Have I Told You Lately That I Love You" was played on the sound system and, as part of the recessional, "Stairway to Heaven" was played.

A few days later, I took Paul's cremated remains in an oak urn (selected by Sheila) to their home. Sheila greeted me with a hug. I can't say as much for the old beagle: she shook in fear the whole time I was in the house. Sheila was apologetic when she told me the dog didn't like me. I love animals and I wanted to be the dog's friend, but also realized the dog saw me as the guy who'd taken her best friend away. She even cowered as I passed by her towards the door.

A support system is vital to any grief process. It was comforting to know that Paul's family has that support. His best friend Steve and his family wrote a letter to Brendan and Daniel:

Although it is easy to see that we share the same name, we share a whole lot more. Our families have so many wonderful memories. We have run, swam, hiked, biked, walked, skied, jet skied, toasted marshmallows, told scary stories, joked and laughed together. And to these great memories, we have your Dad, Mom and grandparents to be forever grateful. [We] started building a house in Milan 21 years ago. We lived in a tent and had no electricity or water the first summer. Walking around Cedar Pond, I noticed a sign on a camp that said "Finnegan."

"Poor people," I said to Steve, "they don't even know how to spell their own name."

"No," said Steve, "that's Paul's parents, they prefer to spell it that way and think that's the way to spell it!"

Before we knew it, we were skinny dipping on the warm (and not so warm) nights in front of the camp. From then on, Cedar Pond fun became a tradition. And now our families mourn, cry and celebrate Paul's life together...Your Dad was the thread that brought us all together and will keep us together forever.

We have been talking about your Dad a lot lately and would like to share with you some of the fun times that maybe you haven't heard about...The night before [our] wedding all my brothers, Steve and Paul [the best man] went frog hunting...I'm not quite sure why. Well, anyway, everyone came home and went to bed. Your Dad was too polite to ask where he was supposed to sleep so he ended up sleeping on a bean bag chair!

...Your Dad was extremely proud of both of you and loved you more than you could ever imagine. He did not want to leave you and in many ways he never will. You will always be our dear friends and we will have many more fun times together. Always be the very good boys that your father knew you to be. Be happy and enjoy what he shared with you. When you are strong, happy, dignified, moral and fair you will show how much your Dad influenced you.

As time goes on, the pain of grief subsides, albeit slowly. When we lose someone so close to us, we lose a piece of ourselves. Read excerpts of how Sheila deals with her sorrow in this letter to Paul 7 months after his death:

Dear Paul,

I write this letter to you in the very spot that you took your last breath, seven months ago. Sometimes it feels like an eternity, sometimes the images are so fresh and stinging it seems like only yesterday. Today when I picked up Dan at baseball practice, I could have sworn one of the other men resembled you from a distance and for a split second I saw you as plain as day, with your hands in your pockets and moving in your very own style, helping Dan with his swing; an image I viewed and took for granted a hundred times. The recognition that I would never see that image again was brutally painful. You are everywhere and nowhere.

I am so sorry that I took anything for granted, that I didn't take more time with you when I had the chance. I was so naïve that I didn't recognize or denied the visible signs of deterioration. I regret now any moment that I was not by your side; I know you forgive me. I'm working to forgive myself.

I truly believe you are in a better place, you are not suffering nor filled with anxiety and disappointment in your body. On the night you died I made you a serious promise. I told you that it was OK for you to leave, that I would take care of everything, that the boys and I would be all right and that I would finish the job that you and I began together of raising two fine young men. I knew you were fighting to live and I didn't want to let you go. Even so sick, your presence was such a comfort. My words were my last gift to you and I felt confident in them. At the time, I couldn't even fathom what living without you for the rest of my life would mean, but I think on some level I feared and realized that I would be struggling with such an awesome responsibility. As much as our family life was central for both of us, it is even more so for me now.

I think the boys are doing as well as can be expected. We have had and will continue to have our difficulties. They are struggling with anger and confusion and challenging the most significant and traumatic event ever to happen to them by challenging me. I'm not sure what is most difficult for me; making all the decisions and second guessing each of them, meeting the needs of two hurting sons who mean the world to me, or handling all the emotions that surge from deep within all of us. You would be proud of each of their accomplishments and growth, in spite of their very deep and inexpressible pain. The gentle manner in which they are dealing with each other is a magnificent tribute to their strong attachment to you. By their mannerisms, interests, love of life, comfort with people and strength of commitment and character you are living on within them. Someday they will recognize you. I hope you would be proud of me as well. It isn't always possible, but sometimes my non-reactive and loving approach surprised even myself. It is at those times that I feel great relief in your presence. When I am angry with everyone and everything around me, I realize I have far to go and can't recognize your presence anywhere.

We all miss your objectivity, knowledge of just about everything, ease of conversation and security of your presence and sheer involvement. Each day I pray for the strength to carry on and I look to the spirit you've left us with to guide and nurture us through the rest of this journey.

Signs of Paul's presence have appeared more than once since his death. David Roy, his friend and running partner, tells this story:

Paul has been my friend for all my life...All through High School we skied and raced on the school ski team. While in college we were roommates for a year. As we started families, we lived in different areas...[but] every time we [met] it was as if no time had passed.

...Over the years we ran in races together...One of these races...is the eight-mile Mt. Washington Road Race to the top of New England. We ran this race a few times during our running careers. I have always viewed this race and the effort it takes as being almost a spiritual event...I would often think about him when I was running and training for the Mt Washington race of 2000.

On race day...as I stood at the starting line...I thought I would run the race for Paul. I envisioned that he would be on my shoulder for the entire race...There was one thing [he wore that] set him apart...a lime green golf visor. Well as the race progressed and I neared the top...I rounded a corner and there...sitting in the middle of the road was a lime green visor. I was stunned to see the visor not blowing in the wind but just sitting there as if just staring back at me. I went on to finish the race while thinking that Paul was there and had found a way to communicate his presence to me.

Another sign happened on the anniversary of his death. On the night before his death, Sheila telephoned a friend from church to help plan the impending service. Upon entering the house, her friend handed her a CD by Robin Speilberg entitled: "Spirit Songs." The CD happened to be in her jacket pocket and it was beautiful piano music. They listened to the first song entitled, "There's a Spirit in this House." It relaxed Paul, and the title alone gave the woman goose bumps. One year later, Robin Speilberg was playing in town. Sheila knew she was meant to attend that concert, and later explained it helped her make it through the weekend.

On what would have been Paul's 50th birthday, Sheila opened their camp at Cedar Pond. Outside was a rainbow — even though it hadn't rained there. Although some may see these as mere coincidences, Sheila views them as signs that Paul is present.

It's obvious Paul made a big impact on those connected with him. Part of this was because he was non-judgmental. He accentuated the positive. Knowing how he lived has taught me to enjoy the simple pleasures, and never to forget to make a difference, especially to my wife and children. It is my hope that the legacy I leave will be as great as that left by Paul Finnegan.

Heaven's Special Child

The Story of Johnny Hill
1934 – 2000

"The happiness of life is made up of minute fractions — the little, soon-forgotten charities of a kiss or a smile, a kind look, a heartfelt compliment, and the countless infinitesimals of pleasurable and genial feeling."
Samuel Taylor Coleridge

Heaven's Special Child

A meeting was held quite far from earth
"It's time again for another birth"
Said the angels of the Lord above,
"This special Child will need much love."
His progress may seem very slow,
Accomplishments, he may not show,
And he'll require much extra care
From all the folks he meets down there,
He may not laugh, or run or play,
His thoughts may seem quite far away.
In many ways, he won't adapt
And he'll be known as "handicapped."
So let's be careful, where they're sent
We want their life to be content.
Please, Lord, find the "parents" who
Will do this special job for you.
They will not realize right away
The leading role they're asked to play
But with the Child from up above,
Comes stronger faith and richer love.
And soon they'll know the privilege given

In caring for this gift from heaven —
Their Precious Child so meek and mild
Is "Heaven's Very Special Child!"
— Author Unknown

IN THE EYES of the mortal being, Johnny Hill was not supposed to be retarded. On November 6, 1934, as Johnny was being delivered, the umbilical cord got wrapped around his neck cutting off the oxygen to his brain causing irreversible brain damage.

This sad beginning never stopped Johnny from living a wonderfully full life. He came from a proud Catholic family and, thanks to their support, he was able to cope with the cruelty of other children. His mother and father ultimately sent him to the Laconia State School where he was with others like him. It was there where he made many lifetime friends.

As adulthood approached, Johnny took classes to learn independent living. When he received his certificate for completing the studies, it was difficult to discern who was most proud: Johnny or his family.

Eventually, Johnny moved into his own apartment with a roommate. He cleaned, cooked and took the bus to work. One day, his roommate had a terrible seizure and Johnny did exactly as he'd been taught. He remained calm and his call to 911 saved his roommate's life. He brushed the hero talk aside, saying he only did what he was taught to do.

I knew Johnny was special after I received a call from a special needs counselor after Johnny had died. The counselor wanted to know what options the family would have if the state paid for the funeral. When the state pays for a funeral, the services and merchandise are minimal. In fact, Funeral Homes make no money under these circumstances, and often don't break even. Indeed, the service is done as a courtesy. The counselor passed the information I gave him to Johnny's sister, Madelyn. Madelyn was not impressed with the options the state had given her and she called me to arrange to come in and plan a funeral for which she and her family would pay. As she put it: "My brother may have been retarded, but he deserves a decent funeral and I intend to make sure he gets it, regardless of the cost." Being a family of modest surroundings, this gesture speaks volumes about their feelings for Johnny and what he meant to them.

They wanted a funeral which would celebrate Johnny's life. A table was set up to display his numerous medals from Special Olympics competitions. There was a collage of photos of Johnny — one of Johnny posing with Senator Bob Dole during the time Dole was running for President. The family didn't even know Johnny had the photo, let alone that he'd met Senator Dole. They laughed at the very idea of Johnny approaching this powerful Senator and saying, "Let's take a picture together, buddy." Senator Dole undoubtedly had no choice but to oblige.

Madelyn also spoke of Johnny's love of parades and how he would march beside the bands greeting people along the parade route. He loved fairs, summer camps, dancing, skiing, and especially the girls. The people of Concord remember Johnny most for his daily routine on Loudon Road (a very busy street) where he stood at the roadside smiling and waving to the commuters. The regular commuters on Loudon Road looked forward to seeing this gentle and loving soul with his "have a nice day" wave!

Whether you knew Johnny personally or just saw him around town, he had a special way of touching your heart. Jason Fisk, a Loudon police officer, wrote the following letter to Madelyn after Johnny's funeral.

I was so sorry to hear that Johnny passed away. I remember very vividly the day I met him. I was washing the cruiser one summer day when I got the feeling that someone was behind me. As I turned around I saw this elderly gentleman, dressed as sharp as could be, smoking a pipe. He was wearing a Fedora and dark glasses.

I asked him if I could help him and he said, "No," after a pause. I said, "Is everything ok?" And in his soft, kind of childlike voice he said, "Hi! I'm Johnny Hill."

I shook his hand and then knew what kind of special person he was as he looked at the cruiser. With eyes completely wide open and not leaving either the cruiser or my badge, he explained to me that he was a police officer.

I said, "You are?"

He said, "Yes, do you want to see my badge?"

I told him, "Sure," and under his suit coat he showed me a small plastic badge pinned to his belt. The small badge I believe was from Concord Police.

I asked if he wanted to help me but he was content just watching. I showed him the inside of the cruiser and everything in it and asked if his car was similar. I don't remember exactly what was said, something along the line of, "it's in the shop getting fixed." I can remember laughing with him and asked where he was from. He pointed across the street to the trailer, to which I asked if he was Harry Hill's son. He stated yes and said he had to go. As he left, I can remember waiting for a bit then followed him to make sure he got [home].

There were many more meetings in which I saw Johnny. Before he would even see who was shouting, that hand would come up and wave...No matter what was wrong with Johnny, he was still a fine man and I could tell by the way he presented himself that he respected himself and wanted people to respect him. Your family has been blessed by having a brother such as Johnny.

It is said in the Bible that those are God's gifted children and that they can do no wrong. God will take care of Johnny and free him from whatever tribulation he had.

Johnny had very little in the way of material things. There may not have been a lot written about him, and he certainly wasn't going to change the world as we know it, but he touched many lives just by being Johnny.

Perhaps we can all take a lesson from his example. We live only one life. If you want something, ask for it the way Johnny asked Senator Dole to pose for a picture with him. If someone needs your help, help them the way Johnny helped his roommate. If you want to let it all hang out and enjoy each moment, don't be apprehensive about getting involved. Be like Johnny in the parades. As one song puts it: "If you get the choice to sit it out or dance, I hope you dance."

Most importantly, be kind to strangers. You never know who they are or what they are going through. Johnny made hundreds of strangers smile and feel good with his wave. I can see him now in heaven, standing beside St. Peter with his police badge checking I.D.'s at the pearly gates. I'm sure he'll be there to wave us in when our time comes. In the meantime, I'll try to carry on Johnny's tradition of being kind to everyone, even if they don't speak back. His memory as a son, brother, friend and hero will be cherished by all. As Madelyn said in closing her Eulogy for him, "We loved him dearly. Rest in Peace, dear Johnny."

Grace Under Fire

The Story of Helen Robichaud
1934 – 2000

"I think a hero is an ordinary individual who finds the strength to persevere and endure in spite of overwhelming obstacles."
Christopher Reeve

I NEVER KNEW Helen as I would have liked, but I did meet her three times and each time she had a big smile and we carried on as if we'd been lifelong friends. I knew she was special the first time I met her.

She came into the Funeral Home with her daughter, Lynn Cote, to make arrangements for her husband (and Lynn's stepfather) who was in a local nursing home, diagnosed with a terminal brain tumor. The doctors had given him four weeks (at best) to live, and Helen decided to get the funeral arrangements completed before he died so she wouldn't have to deal with those details when the time came.

As we sat down, she asked if we could make arrangements for her funeral as well. I told her we'd do whatever she was comfortable with and began by gathering information about her husband. When I got to our arrangement form, which asks for the spouse's address, I was taken aback. Helen looked at me and calmly said, "Hospice House in Concord." I said, "You live in the Hospice House now?" And she replied, "Yes." She explained that she, too, was terminally ill with cancer and had two months to live. No wonder she wanted to make arrangements for herself as well!

After we completed all the specifics for Mr. Robichaud's funeral, I began asking her for the information I needed for her funeral.

She burst into tears. I decided it would be best to plan Helen's funeral at another time.

After a few weeks, Mr. Robichaud lost his battle for life and I met Helen for a second time, on the day of his funeral. She looked lovely and handled the trauma with dignity and grace.

I took a liking to her that I cannot explain. After the funeral, I called her several times and visited her at the Hospice House on one of my rare days off. My wife, Kelly, and I both went and brought her a box of thick peppermint patties. She loved them.

Although she spoke softly, she seemed to be doing remarkably well. We had a wonderful visit, for almost two hours. Before we left, we made plans to pick her up the following week to take her to lunch at her favorite restaurant. But four days after our visit, she died...peacefully. Another funeral director at our firm, Jeromy Heeter, took the call. Once they told him who died, he put the nurse on hold, turned to me and said, "Eric, I think you should take this call." I got teary-eyed as I was writing the information on the "first call" sheet. I was upset that I didn't get the chance to take her to lunch—she was doing so well! How could I not have seen her failing health? Even a funeral director can be in denial about death.

I insisted on doing everything myself. I was with her from the transfer at the Hospice House, to the embalming and cosmetizing, to the dressing and casketing. I wanted her to look as beautiful on the outside as she was on the inside. With God's help, I accomplished that goal.

Despite the appearance of this sweet, gentle woman, it turned out she'd been a truck driver! I had pictured her more as a school teacher. Not that some woman truckers aren't gentle and sweet, but I would venture to say that the majority don't show their soft side that often. In fact, I know some younger woman truckers who would snap my neck if I even remotely suggested they were gentle and sweet.

But Helen had a rare quality of combined gentleness and toughness. She used this quality throughout her life and was able to live an unusual and wonderful existence. When she first started in the trucking business, a New Hampshire Reporter wrote an article about her entitled, *"Cross Country Trucker - Gear Grabbin' Grammy"*. Here are excerpts from that story:

Her daughter calls her "Gear Grabbin Grammy". Helen Robichaud's nickname is well deserved. On May 8, the Milan resident was granted her New Hampshire tractor trailer driving license. Helen's husband Al taught her to drive their 1983 Freightliner while she traveled with him in his trucking business.

"If it hadn't been for his patience I would never have made it," Helen says, recalling how after she received a perfect score on the tractor trailer test Al said he knew all along she could do it.

Al had been in the trucking business for 10 years and Helen soon realized that if the romance was to last, she would have to learn to like trucks.

"At first I was afraid to even get in Al's truck. But then he took me on one trip, and I was hooked," she says.

As soon as she had passed the road test, Al popped the question and got himself a great traveling companion. As they were trucking around the country, Helen began to wonder what it would be like to drive the truck.

"Al was thrilled over the idea," she says.

He devised a unique method for teaching her to drive. He made a gear shift model by inserting a wire into a slit in the plastic cover of an empty Cheeze Ball can. Clothes pins were attached to the wire to represent a splitter. The splitter is like a trigger located on the shift knob which has to be pulled simultaneously as the shift lever is thrust into another gear. This engages a second transmission system with eight close gearing stages. It permits a 400 HP engine to bring a 40 ton load up to highway speeds. From fifth low to highway high requires eight precisely timed shifts — a definite challenge to the coordination.

While on the road and in motel rooms, Helen practiced shifting with her Cheeze Ball can and used an exerciser to strengthen her hand and wrist.

"When Al felt I was ready, he let me try driving on back roads," Helen says. "I gave him some pretty rough rides."

Until she began learning to drive the tractor trailer, she had not even mastered an ordinary standard shift.

"Now, believe it or not, I'm handling 13 speeds," she says.

While on the road, they work hard, she says. For recreation, they play cards and Trivial Pursuit and between loads they take long walks.

"We both love sight-seeing," she says.

They carry only non-perishable freight so they can shut down when road conditions are bad.

"They call us the 'fair-weather twins', "Helen says.

Most of their freight is heavy equipment like bulldozers, tractors and cranes. They even delivered a portable jail to Yuma, Arizona once.

"It was 108 degrees the day we delivered that jail," Helen recalls.

The hottest day, though, was in a place called Giles Bend, Arizona when the temperature hit 117 degrees.

One job Helen found particularly exciting was the delivery to Kennedy Airport of a $6,000,000 satellite bound for Japan.

"We had special security and a police escort," she says.

Helen feels truck driving with her husband is a good experience. Male truck drivers are "very respectful" toward her, she says.

"Here on the East Coast, female truck drivers often drive or own their own rigs," Al says.

"I never intend to lose my femininity," Helen says, explaining that she is careful to keep her hair looking neat and wears earrings.

(Reprinted from the Berlin Reporter)

In a eulogy to her mom, Lynn sums up the essence of what Helen gave to those around her before she died:

We had so many wonderful hours and days together, and I feel that we said everything that needed to be said to each other. However, now that you are gone, I want to share with the people here today a few of the many things that you have taught me and shown me in the past few months.

COURAGE — Al was diagnosed with brain cancer last April. He had had severe headaches for several weeks. You got him to many doctor's appointments and the doctors all told you it was just an ear infection, but you knew better. You insisted he have a cat scan, against the doctor's wishes and you were right - he had a brain tumor. Because of your courage and strength he had 8 more months of life in which you did everything possible to maintain his quality of life, dignity and wonderful sense of humor. Your unbelievable courage gave me the courage to help you these past few months. You ignored your own pain, suffering and illness to take care of the one you loved - and you NEVER complained.

PATIENCE — I sure had a lot to learn in this department! You walked slowly, your words came slowly and it took you forever to do things that I could have done in half the time. You showed me that it doesn't matter at all how long it takes to do something, what matters is that you didn't give up — ever. When you could no longer walk and could barely talk, you NEVER complained - you just smiled and thanked everyone for the least little thing that they did for you and even laughed those last few days!

GRACE — I think this should really have been your name. You never lost your dignity or pride and never melted under the pressure that you had to endure. You left your home in Florida, left your friends behind and lost your husband in December, yet you NEVER complained. You always looked for the positive things in your day. I was always impressed that every day when I came to see you, no matter how sick you felt, you were dressed in a beautiful outfit, complete with matching shoes and lipstick! It made me feel so special.

LOVE — of course, I have always known that you loved us all and you always showed it in so many ways. You were so interested in Chase and Evan's sports accomplishments and academics - you would listen to every detail of a ski race or football or lacrosse game, when I secretly knew that you didn't care for sports. But you did love them so much and for that reason you would listen to and be attentive to anything that I had to say.

My mom wanted everyone to know how much she loved them. Al, Scott, Chase and Evan and all of her brothers and sisters and other family members were loved so much. She also wanted to let her closest friends Marcia and Joyce know that she loved you and will never forget you. Mom, I will never forget you and will always love you.

Courage, patience, grace and love. Four things that we all could use at one time or another. I would add one more thing to Lynn's list: fearlessness.   Whether it was jumping in an 18-wheeler without knowing how to drive a standard transmission, or facing death with dignity and even cheerfulness, Helen displayed an enormous amount of fearlessness.   I shall take that fearless attitude with me through my life's struggles and the everyday obstacles I must face. If I work real hard at it, I may be able to be fearless, selfless, and genuinely happy just like this incredible person. Thank you, Helen, for this gift to me.

The Sawmill Samaritan

The Story of Allan C. Minery Sr.
1928 - 1999

"From what we get, we can make a living;
what we give, however, makes a life."
Arthur Ashe

LOUDON, NEW HAMPSHIRE is a unique little town. It is most famous for the New Hampshire International Speedway (NHIS) where many high profile Bush Series and Winston Cup Auto races are held each year. I, however, know the real reason Loudon is such an awesome town — people like Allan C. Minery Sr. —good old salt-of-the-earth Americans.

Mr. Minery was a simple and gracious man. With five children, Allan and Shirley Minery had plenty to contend with and, although they lived a modest life, it never stopped them from giving to others. In fact, their sawmill was a landmark in town.

Often, when the children were younger, someone would knock on the door during dinner and ask Allan if they could load their truck with sawdust for their animals. First they were offered a place at the dinner table, and then the truck would be loaded. More often than not, Allan refused to take money for the sawdust, especially from needy families in town.

Allan was known for the nicknames he gave to people. One example was Allan's son-in-law who, when Allan came to visit, was evidently always in the bathroom. Allan dubbed him "King" because he was always on the throne! He named one of his grandsons "Duke" (because he was the King's son) and to this day, that boy is still "Duke"! In fact Allan requested that his favorite pocket watch be engraved "To Duke – Love, Gramp" and be given to his grandson after Allan died.

Two of Allan's other grandsons, Billy and Brent, became old enough to work at the sawmill but were still young enough to want to goof off. When they approached their Grandpa together, Allan would say, "Here comes Seymour (See More) and Dooless (Do Less)." He had a fun and loving way that kept the family wondering what he would come up with next.

Allan put everyone else's needs (even animals) before his own. Having a sawmill and a farm, he would wake up early for morning chores. No one was allowed to eat breakfast until all the animals were fed. His niece, Terry Azotea, remembers him working at the sawmill—a big, strong, hulk of a man, yet gentle as a baby with a kindness that made everyone welcome. Someone was always staying at his house because he loved to help people in their time of need. He never worried that he had his own large brood to care for; his concern was for others, not for himself.

When Allan was younger, he'd walk for miles after working all day, to help his sister and brother-in-law build their home. As he aged, his thoughtfulness never waned. If someone showed up at the sawmill while Allan was trying to complete a project, he would stop to help them with what they needed. Even if it took 30 minutes, he would do it cheerfully and he would often refuse payment, saying instead that he was glad to help. On one occasion, Shirley recalled a man who showed up to purchase a considerable amount of lumber. He had a young boy with him to help him load the truck. Once the truck was loaded, Allan told the man what the cost was and as the man was paying, the young boy said, "Dad, does this mean I can't get shoes?" That's all Allan needed to hear to give the whole order to the man at no charge. Shirley jokes today that he was so kind he gave up a weeks pay!. They struggled that week, but as always, God provided.

His goodness did not end at the sawmill. His grandson, Brent (who he called "Brain" because he was always coming up with ideas) remembers being awakened by Grampa one night at about

1:00 a.m. Allan whispered, "Come on son, we're going to pray for Carl." Carl, who was Allan's brother-in-law, lived down the street and was at death's door when Allan went to his brother-in-law's bedside to pray for him.

Even with the simple things in life, his character was clearly visible. He always removed his hat when greeting a lady, and he stood when a lady entered the room.

When he was dying, his focus was on his wife, Shirley. The night before he died, he was talking alone with his daughter Kim and asked "What about your mother? She's going to feel so bad when I go, I feel helpless and so bad for her." The night before he died, his grandson Brent was saying goodbye with a handshake, as they usually did. This handshake was different, though. Grandpa crossed his arms and grabbed onto Brent's left hand with his left hand and Brent's right hand with his right hand. With a tight grip and a gentle squeeze, he winked at his grandson as if to say, "This is it, I'll see you later."

He has been described by his family as the wisest man they ever knew, and this despite his limited education. Even at the sawmill he had an uncanny ability to measure boards with mathematical exactness by using his eyes and his brain. Measuring tapes were unnecessary. Naturally he was good with his hands, and that proved helpful when he refinished his basement for his aging mother-in-law to live in. He designed it exactly the way the inside of her house had been. The refrigerator was in the exact spot from the door, the cabinets were the same, and each room was the same. He wanted her to feel as if she hadn't left her own home. How much more thoughtful can you get?

Allan didn't know what to do with himself when he became ill and couldn't work in the mill anymore. So he started getting up at four in the morning and baking bread! There were fresh loaves of bread all over the kitchen. When anyone came to the house, they always left with a loaf or two. Although he enjoyed his "new line of work" he complained to one of his grand daughters that he had 'woman hands' because they were so smooth and had no dirt on them. He hated that!

Allan's 13 year-old grand daughter, Chelsea, wrote the following:

In your life there is that one person who you can always trust. That one person who you know you can talk to no matter what it is and you know they won't get mad at you. That one person who is serious when they need to be but goofy when you are sad. That one person who is always home when you are not feeling good. That person in my life is my Grandfather. My Grandfather is the kind of person that would literally give his shirt off his back to a man who needed one.

My Grandfather is the sweetest kind of man there is. He had nicknames for everyone. I was Chelstonchew. He always wanted his dinner plate warm and he never took off his hat. He wore blue socks and a checkered shirt. He always smelled like he had just got done working at the sawmill. He had red hair and big hands; his hands are what I remember the most — the curves and lines the size. There is a song called 'Daddy's Hands' but I think it should be 'Grandpa's Hands.' He had blue eyes and a big smile and he loved every one dearly.

My Grandfather was an amazing man. He was always brave. He never looked back. My Grandfather has a place in everyone's hearts and I know that place will always stay in mine.

Chelsea's 10 year old brother, David, said in an article he titled, "What Makes my Grandpa Special":

My Grandfather was a hardworking man. He owned his own sawmill called Minery Lumber. His name was Allan Minery Sr. and he even had a street named after him in Loudon called Minery Road. He stuck with me in the good times and the bad times. He never gave up on me and always had his hopes set on me. He wanted me to do good to others like he did. He wanted me to follow in his footsteps and I want to make the hopes he had for me come true.

Chelsea and David's Mom, Kim, wrote this:

"Throughout the 32 short years that I had the honor of being the daughter of the most wonderful, kind, compassionate, genuine, caring human being that I was blessed to call my father, I am grateful."

She also wrote a poem that she read at his funeral entitled "Memories of my Father":

I have great memories of my Dad,
some make me happy and some make me sad.
I remember growing up and him always working hard,
out in the mill that was out in our yard.
He always would give of himself what he had,
and knowing that when he gave it, it would make him glad.
What a great example that was,
ready to give no matter what the cause.
I remember him when my Aunts would come over,
hiding under the table, was the tape recorder!
I remember the laughter that was always around.
I remember the change being thrown to the ground.
We would all dive to get our share,
those days, it seemed, were without care.
I remember all nicknames he gave everyone,
from the biggest "Guy" to the littlest "Dunn"
I know not one person who has met my Dad,
who has left the house mad, they've always been glad.
He always is willing to give to whoever you are,
from the "take my last dollar" to "here, take my car."
My Dad's had moments in his life,
where he has been thankful for his wife.
He's had the support of his family there,
from the love that we share, to the blessing of prayer.
My Father has faith, there's no doubt about it.
I love him for his strength and the way that he shows it.
I remember my father getting out of bed,
at four in the morning to make his homemade bread.
When we walk in the kitchen you can smell it baking,
"All morning," he says, "That's what I have been making.

You can smell it all that you want with the nose that you've got,
but forget about slicing it when it is hot!"
My memories of you Dad, I will cherish all of my days
with the love you have shown us in a number of ways.
You know the pride that you feel when you look at your family,
and the love that you have, makes you feel glad!
Well, that's what I see and felt when I look up at you, Dad!
I love you!

Every Memorial Day, Allan drove to Connecticut to put flowers on the graves of 12 relatives. This went on for years until his passing in 1999.

He never had a bad word to say about anyone, and he was one of the few who still had faith in his fellow man. He had the ability to make everyone he came in contact with feel really special. His greatest virtue was his honesty. This explains the many pieces of extra lumber he would give to his customers, "just in case a piece or two weren't quite right."

When I reflect on Mr. Minery's life, I think: everyone should treat their neighbors, friends and strangers as Mr. Minery did. He was a shining example of the golden rule. Kim put it best when she said,

"It is said that each of us has been given talents and blessed with certain qualities. This life is the time to share those talents regardless of how insignificant they may seem. We only get one chance in our lives to show others how much we love them, use this time wisely. Life is short; it has a way of passing us by, sometimes without our even being aware. Beyond money, beyond those nice houses, cars and luxuries lies something that is more precious than any material thing, and that is love. What we leave behind when we leave this world and what we will be remembered by will not be what we gained materially. It will be those memories of the love that was shared and with whom it was shared. My father was not worldly; he was, however, blessed with an amazing ability to leave a legacy behind that was focused on love. This has been the greatest gift that I could have ever asked for. I will cherish and honor my father for as long as I live for having given me those qualities to pass on from generation to generation. My father, Allan Clarence Minery Sr. is a man that I am so proud to say, 'That was my Daddy.'"

The Gentle Giant

The Story of Gordon Rowell
1969 – 2000

*"Treasure each other in recognition that
we do not know how long we shall have each other."*
Joshua Loth Liebman

THE ARRANGEMENTS FOR A funeral involve a multitude of details—from the "first call" to committal at the graveside— many things need to happen, usually in a short period of time. To ensure everything goes smoothly, a good funeral director knows to be flexible, accommodating, and patient; especially when a family wants many things done to honor their loved one.

This was the case for the funeral of Gordon (Gordie) Rowell from Bradford, N.H. His older brother, Harry, called me at about 3:00 p.m. on a Tuesday. Earlier that day, Gordie had died peacefully at the age of 30. When we arrived at their little cottage by the lake, Gordie's family and his fiancée, Karin, were there.

Harry was the family "spokesman", so I took the family's requests from him. After answering his questions and explaining the procedure for transferring Gordie from his room to our vehicle, Harry asked if he could assist in carrying Gordie. Harry told me he'd helped Gordie into the house, and he wanted to help carry him out. Letting him do this (which is difficult for a professional, let alone a family member) obviously meant a lot to Harry, and I was pleased to oblige.

I was upset about that "removal" that day, due to an unnecessary pain inflicted on Gordie's grandmother. Before we can take a person from their residence, a qualified nurse (one who works with terminal patients and their families) must sign a death certificate. In this instance, shortly after we arrived, a nurse walked into the house and coldly asked, "Where is the body?"

Gordie's Grandmother was shocked. She looked at me and said, "She just referred to Gordie as 'the body,'" and a tear fell from her face. Since this is my profession, I have heard and referred to a cadaver as "the body" when I haven't known the person's name. But there is no doubt in my mind that it was unprofessional and insensitive for the nurse to make that reference. Gordie's grandmother will never forget it, and neither will I.

Every funeral involves an "arrangement conference", and in the conference for Gordie, there were seven people present besides me— each wanting something different. Every detail was covered, including a catering service for a reception after the funeral. It was obvious everyone cared deeply for Gordie. I could sense the impact he'd had on everyone who knew him.

Gordie had friends from all over the world. His friends from Ireland (Sinead and Jerome) told me Gordon was the most decent person you could meet and was exceptional in every way. Another friend said he had never known anyone with such warmth and loving energy.

By the time the family and friends gathered to celebrate Gordie's life with a memorial service at the Unitarian Church in Concord, N.H., I felt a bond with his family. Hundreds of people came to the service and the line to get in the church was so long, I had to go outside to see where it ended. When I finally reached the end of the line, I saw three large buses which had transported his friends and co-workers from Boston!

As everyone sat (or stood) in silence, Harry got up to speak. He thanked everyone for coming and explained how honored Gordie would have felt. He then asked everyone — in memory of Gordie — to give Gordie a hand and applaud the life he lived. I got goose bumps when everyone stood up and gave Gordie a five minute standing ovation; cheering, whistling and clapping. Who knows how long it might have gone on? Harry had to ask everyone to stop! That was the first and only time I've seen something like that at a funeral. Obviously, Gordie was indeed a special man.

It's fitting that both his brother, Harry, and his best friend, David, each wrote a tribute to Gordie.

From his best friend, David Blake:

Two Things I Remember About Gordon Rowell

I.   We were working at the moving company in those days. It was summer. For some reason, the moving company...kept working the two of us together as a crew...but we weren't complaining. Hard work is better with a friend.

Gordon and I had grown up together...knew the same people to varying degrees, went to the same parties, the same secret spots, the ponds and lakes, all the back roads, the places to take girls. And we both left that town as soon as we got the chance. Now we were in Boston, working at the same moving company, a job our friend and Gordon's brother, Harry helped us get.

Gordon and I had recently come through some shaky times when we met up again that summer. There was the feeling that we had done some wild things, run up against some bad luck, but that things were changing. For four or five days a week, every week for one summer, we carried furniture, sweated, laughed and told stories. Sometimes, at the end of a day, we would take our tips and find a local pub...We never talked about it then – although we talked about a lot of things – but I think we both felt that, despite the hard work, we didn't want these days to end. But that is how it is with friends; you're supposed to have a good time with each other. We'd eat our turkey club sandwiches, drink pints of beer and watch the ballgame. At the end of the night it was, "See you tomorrow." Do it all over again the next day.

II.   Gordon had a mandolin. It was a really fine instrument... Gordon had seen it in a music shop and decided he had to have it. He didn't have enough money at the time, so he gave the guy a down payment with a promise to come back every two weeks until he paid it off...I don't know how long it took him. Two months? Three? But he got it.

Gordon practiced on this thing every night, teaching himself to play. I played a little guitar. Gordon was a better guitar player than me and now he had this mandolin. But none of this was a problem. There wasn't competition or petty jealousies between us...But that was a thing about Gordon...There was an easy quality to our days together. Whether we were lugging some big piece of furniture – some sleeper sofa – up three flights of stairs, driving around town, watching a ballgame, or sitting around playing music, trading songs, there was the sense that everything was as it should be. That life, despite all its snags, disappointments and rough edges, was okay. Gordon was making all this music and I was writing poems in my head to a woman who lived down the street. It was all about song.

But we also knew that this was part illusion, that none of it was permanent. The summer would end, I would go on to graduate school, Gordon would learn how to fly airplanes, fall in love with Costa Rica, etc. But we didn't bitch about it or mention it, we just took as much as we could possibly get.

This is something I never told anybody, at least not until I was asked to speak at a small memorial service for Gordon after he died...but it gets me back to Gordon and his mandolin, which is where I was trying to go in the first place. Occasionally, maybe once or twice a week, when I got to the yard where we met in the mornings to get our paperwork and go out on the job, Gordon would be there waiting, ready to go. I'd climb in on the passenger's side and we'd take off.

Once we were stopped somewhere, safely out of site of that moving camp and the other movers, Gordon would reach behind the driver's seat and, without saying anything, pull out his mandolin case, holding it by the handle and shaking it over his head like some prize fighter holding up his hard-won championship belt. And I knew right then that we would bust our asses that day to finish the job fast, and that rather than going back to the yard to see if there was more work or somebody who needed help, we were going to play music. And it probably speaks to the difference between us, which, after all, were as important to our friendship as our similar tastes, that after an hour or two of this Gordon would start to feel the guilty tug of responsibility and pack it up to head back to the yard to whatever labor was waiting there.

And from his brother, Harry Rowell:

My Brother Gordon

It takes a lot of courage to follow a dream; especially one that you may have had for a while, never forgotten about but never acted on either. My brother Gordon always wanted to fly. When we asked him what he wanted for his thirtieth birthday he told us: flying lessons. So on December 2, 1999, that is what we got him.

The next seven months were busy ones for Gordon. In addition to a full workload and a busy social life, he made great strides toward his pilot license. He was a quick study, and was on the verge of taking his first solo flight. Through it all, he continued to play his music and he even made a return trip to Costa Rica with his long time girlfriend. They had wonderful news for us upon their return; they were engaged.

Gordon served as best man at my wedding. In fact, he lived with my wife-to-be and me in Boston for three years, before we moved to the west coast. Most people do not get to live with their siblings once they leave the nest. I was lucky. I not only got to live with Gordon but I got to work with him too.

It was amazing to see him come into the company I had worked at for years. In a very short time he had truly endeared himself to all of his coworkers and instituted himself into the very fabric of the Gentle Giant [moving company]. His rapid rise to a position of responsibility and respect was testimony to his true leadership ability. But anyone can lead; the real question is, will people follow them? Gordon's friends would follow him anywhere.

Gordon had a very special way about him. His easygoing nature, quiet dignity and the true respect he had for people were all apparent when he looked you square in the eyes, and with a slight smile and a bit of a nod, genuinely listened to what you were saying. He was always a true peacemaker, and I have never met another person who was as cool in any type of pressure situation.

In June, Gordon called me at my home in Oregon. He had been diagnosed with cancer. Thirty years old. Non-smoker. Lung cancer. The doctor had given him six months. I felt like I had been shot. But his voice was, as always, strong, resolute, and very brave. I remember him being most concerned about telling our family.

Gordon's family and friends circled the wagons. If there was ever a greater group effort, motivated by love, to help save an individual from a virtual death sentence I have never heard about it.

77

I went back east and back to work at the company a few days a week to be close. In the months that followed, though at times Gordon's strength was not 100%, I never saw his hand shake or embrace falter; never once.

There is one story, which in my mind, sums up all the courage, humor and grace that Gordon exhibited during those difficult months. He was always studying his flight study books or reading his pilot magazines and if he wasn't, they were at his bedside. One day he saw me looking through some of them and he told me that he studied them as hard as he did because the last thing he wanted to do was beat cancer only to take his Cessna into the trees with all of us there watching his first solo flight. We both laughed as hard as we had in a long time.

When my brother Gordon died on November 28, 2000, and it was time to make arrangements, we all decided his memorial service should be on his birthday. Looking back, it was a purely selfish decision; none of us wanted to be alone on that day, but I doubt that anything so selfish had ever turned into something so beautiful. There were more than four hundred people there on December 2, 2000 for my brother Gordon; forever thirty, forever brave.

His closest friends celebrated another memorial service a day after the large service in Concord. This service, however, took place in the small white country church in the center of Bradford, NH, where Gordie and Karin were to be married.

Many of Gordon's friends and family honored him by speaking at his memorial services. None, however, showed more courage in doing so than his mother, Alison, and his fianceé, Karin.

Alison spoke of the way Gordon lived his life and how he enjoyed his friends, family, and life experiences to the fullest. She also talked about how, since he was a little boy, he was always the one to make the peace between others.

Karin spoke about how, on several occasions, Gordon had saved other people's lives. She said he was humble about being a lifesaver; almost as if it was no big deal that others were alive because of his decisive actions.

After the services, many people said they had come to pay their respects to Gordon and to be there for Gordon's family when, in fact, seeing Alison and Karin rise to the occasion and hearing them both speak so eloquently, they felt Gordon's loved ones were there for them.

If I could touch as many lives as Gordie Rowell and make such a positive difference in my world, I would be honored. Thirty years is not a long time to be here. Gordie made every day count and he left this world in a better condition than when he found it.

When I think of Gordie's family and all the families that have suffered a loss, I try to remember the old saying, "It is better to have loved and lost then never to have loved at all." May we all receive the blessing of life in a way the Lord has planned, and may we stop to appreciate those we truly love, and make the world a better place — for the day will come when we all need to say good-bye.

"Carter's Blessings"

The Story of J. Carter Brown
1987 – 2001

*"To everything there is a season and a time
to every purpose under the heavens"*
Ecclesiastes 3:1

LIFE WAS JUST BEGINNING for J. Carter Brown, a happy, outgoing, vibrant and handsome 13 year old, whose life ended in a most unusual way and at an already difficult time for his family.

The son of a certified social worker/minister, Billy and his wife Nancy, Carter was family oriented and was very involved in his church's activities. Living in Hopkinton, New Hampshire, he enjoyed the life of a small town boy and had the good fortune of belonging to the South Congregational Church in Concord. At a young age, Carter learned the importance and value in helping others, so he was more than willing to volunteer his time and services with a smile on his face. In fact, he was the first and *only* male member of the church's Guild!

Among the activities which Carter enjoyed, a favorite was visiting his grandparents in Virginia. "Cold Spring" —the 860-acre family farm—gave Carter and his little sister, Elizabeth, freedom to roam. He loved to ride an old green tractor his Grandpa had bought years earlier. Every visit was a happy adventure, although not every visit was for pleasure.

On May 4, 2001, Carter's grandmother, Elizabeth, died at the age of 81. Because he knew where his grandmother was, Carter was in peace about her death, but was naturally sad that he'd never see her again. Her funeral was held on May 7, 2001 at 2:00 p.m. After returning to the farm, Carter put his Grandma's memorial folder in his pocket, changed into his jeans, and headed off for a ride on his favorite tractor.

Because Carter was a regular pro with the tractor, no one worried about him. As time went by, from minutes to hours, everyone figured he needed to be alone for awhile. But after several hours, Billy and Nancy figured he'd lost track of time, so they decided to walk the farm to find Carter riding atop the tractor. I wish that's what they had found. Instead, they found the tractor tipped on its side on a hill and Carter lay dead 20 feet away. The tractor had evidently rolled 40 yards down an embankment, fatally injuring Carter's internal organs, before resting on its side a few feet away.

I was called by a funeral director at McCoy Funeral Home in Blacksburg, Virginia. He had just finished the funeral of Carter's grandmother, and now he had to bring her dead 13-year-old grandson to the Funeral Home for preparation and transportation back to New Hampshire. While he was incredulous about what had happened, he managed to explain the situation to me. He told me how polite and handsome Carter was, and that he was just talking to him in the limousine a few hours earlier. We were both concerned for the family, but especially Carter's dad. We asked each other, "How could he lose his mother and then, on the day of her funeral, lose his only son at the age of 13?" Life didn't seem fair. Despite our sadness, we knew we had a job to do and we tended to the business of ensuring a smooth transition from Virginia to New Hampshire, where I would begin to coordinate a fitting tribute and farewell for Carter.

Once the travel logistics had been arranged, I set up with Billy and Nancy, to meet the following day. It's impossible to explain how I felt when I looked into their eyes. I was unmistakably heartbroken.

Their love for God was clearly evident after just a few moments. I knew they would appreciate the support, love and prayers they would get from the community, and I knew that because of their faith, they would make it through this dark passage.

While making the funeral arrangements, I was wearing a "paratrooper wings" lapel pin and as I was saying goodbye to the family, Billy pointed to my "wings" and said, "I want to thank you for wearing these. You have no idea what it means to me." He explained that Carter had wanted to be a Ranger, Paratrooper, Green Beret or Navy Seal. Somehow, my being a former paratrooper seemed appropriate to Billy and he was comforted knowing that Carter would probably want it no other way.

His family believes he would have pursued the elite military or the ministry. Even at 13, Carter was known for his compassion, patience, understanding, determination, optimism and a gift for teaching. In the fall of 2001, four months after Carter's death, his friend, Patrick McNichols wrote a tribute to Carter, excerpted here:

May, 2001, easily the worst month of my life. One of my best friends, Carter Brown had been killed in a tractor accident...My mom loved Carter, so that morning I woke up to her yelling and frantically crying [and] I couldn't imagine what happened. After my mom finally got the words out, I don't know how I stayed conscious.

Naturally, I didn't believe what had happened and figured I'd go to school to take my mind off things...big mistake. After I walked into Spanish class, took a look at where he sat, I lost it...The next thing I knew I was in Guidance surrounded by about 15 other people. I just [sat] there bawling, and receiving hugs from anonymous people. After I had calmed down slightly, I met...with the minister of our church. It was a neat surprise, and it felt good.

My friend, Josh, and I decided to invite several of Carter's friends to my house. The main theme that day would be working on my tree house. Carter had previously been over once a week to help build, and he loved it. Some of his friends didn't know the difference between a nail and a screw, but who cares? My second goal that day was to make room for a few laughs and I achieved that too. When the day was over we had finished putting up all the electrical, the upper porch railing, windows and shingled most of it.

It was probably the most fun anyone could have had given the circumstances.

That day obviously was not the end of my pain. It hadn't hit me seriously yet, and I still expected Carter to say hi to me in the halls and come over to work.

The day would come when I was off to a baseball game in Bradford. Carter loved to play catcher and already had some great catches out in left field. So, simply driving in the car, it hit me, he wasn't going to be there! He wouldn't be my catcher when I came in to pitch! What do you mean? I ended up just watching the game in tears along with some other teammates.

The biggest thing, though, has been the fact that Carter was a climber, a good one, and he took it seriously, always safe. Now up until he died, I didn't know the difference between a wired stopper and a technical cam. The main thing is, I didn't like it and thought it wasn't worth dying on the side of a cliff for. Now, things have changed. I have 14 books about climbing, have most of the necessary gear, and want a ticket to Nepal! My thoughts have changed about climbing, from suicide to getting out and enjoying your company and the final view...I believe the only way I could be this into it is that Carter must have given his passion to me...and every time I climb I feel close to him. I feel like he is a rope length away, belaying me. I intend to hold his talent until I simply can't do it anymore.

Carter was determined and enjoyed perfecting certain things. Well, he perfected how he treated people and nature, that's for sure. I am so glad I got to know this great humorous character while I had the chance, and I am thrilled about what he gave me. What a great kid.

Hundreds from the Hopkinton and Concord communities came to the church to say their last good-bye to a boy who seemed well beyond his years. In his eulogy to Carter, Irvin Gordon, one of Carter's coaches spoke to all the young boys in the sanctuary that day imploring them to carry on Carter's example, both as an athlete and as a person.

...I am but one of many coaches, teachers and parents who, during the past several years, have had the privilege of knowing and working with Carter.

Carter was, over several seasons, a stalwart defender on his soccer team. With his height, keen sense of the action...and willingness to run until he dropped, Carter was an anchor of the defense. But while Carter was a force to be reckoned with on the soccer field, it was Carter the Baseball Player I will remember best.

The sweatiest, dirtiest, most thankless and arguably the most difficult position on a youth baseball team – and the position that offers, on each pitch, the greatest potential for extreme personal embarrassment – is, I believe most would agree, the catcher, [and] Carter was the Rockets' primary catcher.

Carter brought to that role the same quiet determination, gentle and respectful manner, obsession with improving his skills and justifiable pride in his progress and accomplishments that...he demonstrated so abundantly in his family, his church work, his rock climbing, his music and acting and the many other endeavors he undertook.

And what *enthusiasm!* On the Thursday before his accident, the Rockets played a pre-season scrimmage game against the Hopkinton Hawks. Carter was to play left field for the first three innings, and to catch the Rockets' fastest pitcher over the last four innings. In the second inning and again in the third inning Carter made difficult catches in left field, the latter a running shoetop grab of a sinking liner headed up the left-center field alley, for certain extra bases. I will never forget Carter's request, as he ran into the team dugout after the second catch, flashing that beautiful smile: *"Hey, can I stay out there for some more of those?"*

On the day following Carter's accident, the Rockets gathered at the home of one of his teammates, under a cloud of quiet disbelief. In reminiscing about Carter there were – in that enviable compartmentalization that Youth allows – both tears and laughter. After some discussion among themselves, Carter's teammates announced that, to honor Carter, they had decided to purchase a special bat (the "Carter Brown" bat) – not to be placed in some trophy case or forgotten corner – but instead to be carried in the team bat bag and to be called upon when, over the coming season, a key hit might be needed. The boys announced, further, that at the end of the season they intend to present the bat to Carter's family, in his memory and honor. So, Nancy, Elizabeth and Billy, you can expect that "Carter's Bat".

There are not words...to convey adequately to Nancy, Elizabeth and Billy – either our gratitude for your sharing Carter with us, or our sense of loss at this time. We can, however...all cherish the wonderful memories Carter has left with us, and aspire, ourselves, to the example of grace, zeal, diligence and compassion that he demonstrated so generously in his young life.

At times like this, we turn to our family, our friends and our faith to sustain us. We may draw strength, also, from the wisdom of poets and philosophers who, over the centuries, have sought to understand the inexplicable caprice by which Fate can visit grief upon us. One such was the poet A.E. Houseman who, in his poem "To an Athlete Dying Young," reminds us that, while Carter may no longer be with us in some physical, tangible sense, we will forever be blessed with the unblemished memory of his youthful zeal and accomplishment.

So boys, as we leave this service, let us remember the example that Carter set for all of us, and strive to do justice to that example.

(Remarks of Irvin D. Gordon at the Celebration of the Life of J. Carter Brown at the South Congregational Church, U.C.C., Concord, NH, on May 12, 2001.)

Besides being an outstanding athlete, Carter was a wonderful big brother to Elizabeth. He instinctively knew what to do and say to calm any situation, especially those involving her. When Carter was seven years old, he protected and loved her with a discernment not seen in some adults. As the story goes, Elizabeth was afraid to sleep at night because "monsters" were coming into her room. This seemed to be an ongoing problem for her parents until Carter decided to put his Power Ranger figures on her windowsills, explaining to her that they would protect her from the monsters. From that night on, Elizabeth slept like a baby with no worries or fears of anything harming her while she was sleeping.

Somehow, Carter was a kid and an adult at the same time. During a Sunday school class when he was in sixth grade, the teacher asked if there were any prayer concerns. Carter wanted to pray for his R.V. Finding this a bit odd, the teacher gently asked Carter why he wanted the class to pray for his R.V. He told the class that the R.V. was to carry his family across the country on a trip that summer. What sounded at first like a ridiculous request, ended up being quite important, and for a good reason. His wit was unparalleled by anyone his age.

Corrine LaJoie, one of Carter's guidance counselors explained his personality this way, "Carter would come to guidance whenever he thought there was an issue that he might affect for the better. Usually he had already processed the possible solutions and just needed a sounding board. Extraordinarily self-reflective, sensitive to other's needs, articulate and principled, Carter was wonderfully unusual. I feel enriched to have known him."

Carter stood up for the underdog, even when it wasn't popular to do so. His principles were more important than his popularity. As a young girl, Katie Meyer explains, "Carter and I rode the same bus to school. There was one kid who the high school kids would make fun of when this boy got on the bus. One day Carter stood up to them and asked them to be nice. He told them to treat the boy the same way they would like to be treated. What he did was very nice, brave and kind." Like his friend Megan Cantara said, "Carter Brown was always a nice guy to everyone. He was never mean or disrespectful and I will always remember what a great person he was."

Carter was a great person because he possessed the qualities that make a person great. There was a beautifully framed collage on display at Carter's funeral with pictures showing Carter at camp. What brought this particular collage to life, however, was a poem positioned in the middle of all the photographs, written by J.T., a camp counselor who was also a close friend.

What Are The Qualities of Life?

What are the qualities of life?
It can be shared forever, but cannot be kept forever.
When given to another, it brings great joy to all; when
Taken, the anguish for many is great.
It is sometimes maintained by less than a thread of a

String and sometimes lost despite the hopes of millions.
Its frailty and end are obvious, but its strength and limits endless.

So share your life with me while we are together
so we can create that which will bring joy to others.
When this life is over, let the meaning of our lives be
found not on a list of accomplishments, but in the hearts
and souls of the people with whom we shared our fragile existence.

Let our lives not be measured so much by what we
did for others, but by what we helped others do for themselves.

Carter's family sent special Thanksgiving cards to their friends on the Thanksgiving after his death. In it, there was a story entitled "About 'Carter's Blessing'"

On Thanksgiving Day, 1995 we gathered with friends and family around a table filled with delicious food prepared with loving hearts and hands. As is our custom, we joined hands in anticipation of saying Grace. This day, Carter asked if he might offer the blessing. With heads bowed we listened as this simple blessing flowed beautifully and powerfully from Carter's heart. We share this with you as a way of honoring Carter's kind and generous spirit.

CARTER'S BLESSING

Thank you God for the food in front of us
The friends around us
And the love inside us.
AMEN

From the time Billy told me of Carter's ambition to be an elite military soldier, I felt a posthumous bond with him. Every picture I saw of him I reflected on my own childhood. I even felt a guilty envy because he always had a huge smile on his face. Pictures of him rock climbing and rappelling reminded me of the joy I'd had when I did such things in the military. Not only did Carter do these things, he did them well. He was a natural.

I asked Billy and Nancy if it was okay if I placed an Army "Ranger" sweatshirt of mine in Carter's casket. Billy said Carter would have thought that was "awesome". I was honored that they allowed me to share in a small way. I wish I'd had the pleasure of sharing his company when he was alive.

A year after Carter's death, his family had a small ceremony in dedicating his headstone. That dedication follows:

Dedication of J. Carter Brown's Headstone
Old Hopkinton Cemetery
May 11, 2002

Prayer of Invocation:

Oh God, we know that your heart was the first to break as we began this journey of living our lives without Carter We gather this day to celebrate the journey of the past year as we have learned together that indeed, "A Broken Heart Still Beats." We have felt your Spirit in our heavy sighs, our tears, our hugs, in the kind notes of remembrance, in the countless memories and stories shared at dinners, ball fields, and in conversations throughout this community.

We ask for your Presence today, as we mark a point in time and a place on this earth where we can focus our hearts and minds on the gifts You have given to the world. Carter was a gift to us. Help us be mindful that we are gifts to each other. As our lives unfold, assure us of your constant presence, enriching, renewing and sustaining our lives. Hold us in Your Loving Hands, Oh God; give us comfort and courage in this time and forever more. In Christ's name, we pray. Amen.

The Story of the Stone:

In the weeks and months that unfolded following Carter's death, Nancy and I began to focus on the task of how to choose a marker for Carter's gravesite. Ideas and images came and went as we tossed around the seemingly impossible notion that any marker would be adequate to the task. When you live in a presence of such a spirit as Carter, you are reminded that there is a balance of both the positive and the negative in his energy. So the ideas that came to mind included a massive monolithic stone rising to great heights with writings filling all exposed sides recounting amazing stories where Carter had certainly astounded his parents and sister with acts of wisdom beyond his years. The balancing images included leaving the spot marked with essential information of name and dates as a reminder to us and especially to him that life was a humbling experience.

As we talked and reflected on what would be the right marker, we began to visit cemeteries in the vicinity. The stones we were most attracted to were those that told a story about the person. As we all know, Carter loved to tell stories, so we began to focus on words and symbols that would tell as much of Carter's story as we could.

The Black Granite, which comes out of Africa, was chosen because of its vibrancy and energy. The Blackness stands in contrast, not in opposition, to the New Hampshire gray granite as a reminder of Carter's uniqueness and his resolve to be who he was in the presence of others who were different from him.

We chose the wide base to celebrate Carter's being grounded in his life in his community. He loved being here, and he loved being on the family farm in Virginia. In his time, he was well loved by us, and by all of you. From this solid base he was beginning to soar upward in his life, as the tapered shape of the stone captures.

As Carter was making his way through his life, he was learning to meet challenges in his way, with his unique gifts. Nowhere in his life did the confluence of his gifts and the world's challenges meet with greater excitement and passion for him than in the experience of rock climbing. So, his stone had to have the draw of a 'good rock' as Carter would say. The stone needed rough edges, hand holds, small ledges for a balancing point, a good place to set an anchor, and some flat spots for resting and sitting a while to admire the view and restore energy for the next leg of the climb. We hope the stone is inviting and that we all will be drawn here to climb, rest or reflect as we have need.

The words to choose seemed a daunting task. Beyond the name, "J" for Jesse, after his grandfather, and "Carter," chosen from an old family name rooted in Virginia, what else can tell the story? You put dates on a marker and let people do the math. The reality of "just shy of his 14th birthday" emerges as your heart and mind can allow. This is part of the story, but what else?

Our memory of Carter is always colored by his brightness. He had the gift of a bright countenance, and his smile was his ticket into your heart. It was the opening line of his story from day one, and the theme was repeated in countless scenes and encounters. Bright, positive energy accompanied him and he shared that gift with us.

Carter had a heart that was wired to the world in a special way. He was sensitive to his world, and at times he was way too sensitive for his own good or ours. He could be stubborn, and at times be a royal pain to those around him. Through all of his sensitivity and his insensitivity, ultimately what came through was his kindness. He had a gentle way about him that was a combination of his innate kindness and the kindness he learned from his family and the community. Most of his learning about kindness came from his own struggles when he encountered a world that was different and unkind to him. At times Carter had a right to become bitter and withdrawn, but thanks to a loving community of caring people and a Church family where he could be different and have those differences celebrated, Carter's kind heart grew and became stronger.

Friends were important to Carter. He worked harder at learning how to be a friend and then how to sustain friendships than any young man we knew. He was not always successful at being the kind of friend he wanted to be, but he did always work at it. And from the stories some of you have told us, he was beginning to get the friendship thing pretty well.

Carter loved us as his family. He was not a perfectly loving son or brother. He would act at times in ways that were selfish and even at times hurtful to us. No matter what the circumstance or the power of his conflict with each of us, at the end of the day, Carter would return to the loving relations seeking reconnection in a loving manner. He taught us and we taught him that loving in a family does not mean agreeing all the time. Loving within a family meant and means now, respecting and honoring each other as a unique gift to the world.

On the side of this stone we have affixed a medallion that recognizes Carter as a tissue donor. Carter was determined to be one of the good guys – a hero. The morning after his death, we were given the opportunity for him to become just that. We were contacted by the Virginia Life Net organization asking if we would be willing to allow Carter to be a tissue donor. Carter's organs were too injured in the accident to be useful for organ donation, but some of his bones and skin, his corneas and other tissues could be useful. So in his death he provided the means by which others could once again see or heal from burns or cancer surgery. We were sure Carter wanted us to let this be one of the ways he was to live on. We have chosen to put the medallion here on his stone because we know Carter would want to encourage others to make the same choice. This is the story of the stone.

Soon we will be singing, and we will be leaving this place. And what next? Our family and this community have now come through a year without Carter's physical presence in our lives. You have sustained us in ways that we will never be able to count and our gratitude to all of you is beyond measure. In marking this anniversary, we would like you to take parts of Carter with you. We invite you to take his brightness and mix it with your own. Take his kindness and enhance your own capacity to be kind in the world. Be caring in a mindful and intentional way, and remember that Carter worked hard at being a friend. Our hope is that we can all become more loving in ways that respect and honor all people and places where growth and openness to creativity are nurtured.

The final prayer at the dedication of Carter's stone sums up the essence of a beautiful person. Carter's example has reminded me that patience, kindness, and respect — along with a dedication to pursue excellence in everything — is the true measure of a man's character.

The Ice Princess

The Story of Amy Alice Huckins
1961 – 2002

"Let us be of Good Cheer, remembering that the misfortunes hardest to bear are those that will never happen."
James R. Lowell

AMY HUCKINS WAS a happy-go-lucky 40-year-old with a beautiful home, a loving husband of 18 years, great friends, and the desire and ability to ice skate anytime she could. An accomplished figure skater, Amy never missed the chance to watch a figure skating competition or be on the ice herself. Amy was particularly excited about the tickets she'd recently received to attend the figure skating competition at the upcoming Winter Olympics in Salt Lake City, Utah. That's all she talked about with her husband, Chuck, as she flashed her beautiful smile and bubbled over with excitement in anticipation of that day.

Cold New England weather didn't bother Amy, nor did driving in difficult winter conditions. So, on January 17, 2002, she ate breakfast and, before she left for work, she gave Chuck a hug and kiss good-bye and went downstairs. She ran back upstairs and gave him a hug and kiss again as he sat in his chair and said, "I just wanted to kiss you one last time before I leave."

Right down the road from her home, Amy came to a stop sign. Though she tried, the car would not stop due to the treacherous icy condition of the road. A neighbor, driving his truck on the road perpendicular to where Amy was, could not stop either and his truck slammed into her car, killing her. Ice was something that shaped Amy's entire existence and it was the very thing that cost her her life.

Chuck, Amy's mother, Allie and Amy's sister, Lisa, walked into Bennett Funeral Home unexpectedly to make funeral arrangements. I'd read about the accident in the newspaper, but now I was to become very involved in providing a fitting tribute to such a beautiful life so well lived. In doing so, I had the pleasure of meeting some truly wonderful people. One of them was Amy Valenti, one of Amy's best friends, who lived in Dover, Delaware. The following are excerpts of her thoughts from the day she met Amy, to the day she lost her "Kindred Spirit".

It was sometime the first week of October 1980 when Amy and I met...in the study lounge of our dormitory. We were the only two there that night and of course not much studying got done. We got to talking and of course laughing and that night I realized I had met a truly unique person.

There are so many ways to describe Amy: generous, caring, loving and most importantly, devoted; to name just a few. I often told my husband and friends that I had to be VERY careful what I said to Amy (imagine having to be careful what to say to your friend...) for many times things would show up in the mail. For example, shortly after my grandmother died, I was on the phone with Amy and...mentioned that grape soda always reminded me of sitting and talking on the porch of the big farmhouse with my grandmother. Less than 24 hours later, [I got] a package from Amy: A six pack of grape soda! Another example was when I told Amy how much I missed eating a New Hampshire apple (like no other apple in the world!). Two or three days later [I got] a package of two-dozen tasty Macintosh New Hampshire apples. My last birthday gift from Amy, one I will always treasure, is a box of 64 Crayola crayons complete with its own built-in sharpener. Such a simple gift but an item I had never owned as a child. Amy couldn't let me live without ever owning one of my own.

Whether staying up late in our dorm rooms or as we got older, on the phone, we talked, laughed, giggled, cried, but most importantly told each other over and over how special we were to one another. When Amy died a part of me really did die with her. I have no one to share our silly little stories with, and when you've known someone for almost 22 years...there are a lot of stories. Like the time we got caught deflowering the lilac bush at UNH,...the wonderful sleigh ride complete with falling snow, and...our trip to the 2001 US National ice-skating Championships and meeting Miss Peggy Fleming. I always knew that my dear friend would be there for me when I needed her, good times and bad. She was one of the first I called when each of my sons was born, and she was one of the first I called when my brother was killed. Always...Amy was my "always" friend. Living out of state when my brother died, I had no one to watch my then 10-month-old son while I attended his wake and funeral. It was Amy who came through for me despite recuperating from knee surgery. When I was in the hospital for a week due to a pregnancy-related illness, it was Amy who called me more than anyone else. She was the one who sent me coloring books, markers, playing cards and of course a Cosmopolitan magazine so as to keep my mind off my illness. Amy ALWAYS knew how to cheer me up, ALWAYS knew what to say, and was ALWAYS willing to do all she could to help me in any situation.

About 11 years ago, Amy and I realized we had more than just a strong friendship. Maybe it was the same name thing, but one day I told her we were each other's kindred spirit and from that day on that is what we started calling each other. I once wrote to her that we would be each other's "K.S." till death do us part. In the months since her death, I have come to realize that I will NEVER have another person in my life like Amy. Sure, I'll have wonderful friends who I will treasure, but as we all know "kindred spirits" cannot ever be replaced.

Amy had a wonderful way with words. She would bring me to tears and laughter with her writing. In one of my last phone calls with her, we were discussing the skater, Michelle Kwan, and an outfit she had worn. It was absolutely breathtaking. We were trying to come up with a name of the color she wore. It was a very pale light blue with some silver tones woven throughout the material. In a split second Amy described it as "Heaven's Glow." Little did we know a few weeks later my Kindred Spirit would be glowing down on all of us from Heaven. Does Crayola take suggestions for new colors? Oh, how I miss my dear friend.

I always knew life was full of simple pleasures. The little things that Amy did for her friend were simple, yet priceless. Even a small gesture makes the difference between a good day and a really bad day. I was very touched by Amy's thoughtfulness and her ability to make someone feel "just right."

Amy was also very close to her family. On the flight to New Hampshire to attend Amy's funeral, her half sister Amanda wrote about her sister. Excerpts follow:

> Amy had (gasp, past tense. Long pause. How can someone so alive not be alive? It's unreal.) a huge heart — room for each of us here today.
>
> Amy showed she cared...openly, with expression like very few people I have ever met. [Her] love...gushed out of her like a waterfall.
>
> Amy was supportive and encouraging of everything I ever did — and genuinely enthusiastic with her support. Amy's enthusiasm was contagious — and fun and funny.
>
> Amy taught me so much about life...She was one of the greatest teachers I ever had. She taught me to tie my shoes on a summer vacation on Cape Cod; helped me learn to read; taught me how to braid my hair; gave me my first glass of wine — with ice cubes, no less — then took me for my very first drive (yes, in that order) and, not surprisingly in hindsight, after I successfully pulled back into her driveway I...hit the garage door. But, that led to an even more important lesson: forgiveness. Amy and Chuck taught me to forgive and laugh at the mistakes in life, which inevitably happen and can be repaired.
>
> Amy sent me her dress from her honeymoon to wear to my first formal dance in high school. At the awkward age of 13, I wore that dress with confidence because it was Amy's — she was there for me, teaching me that if I felt beautiful, then I was beautiful through a medium we both adored — by letting me borrow her "cloe," Amy's childhood word for the singular of "clothes."
>
> Amy took me for my first makeover at a department store beauty counter — during a one day shopping spree financed with a pay check Chuck had misplaced and found the night before. Amy taught me to live life and enjoy the moment — particularly the fun whimsical moments, which she found or created more often than most people. But, she also taught me to savor the memories — I still have the lipstick.

Amy went with me to tour the college I decided to attend. Her vote of confidence and advice were factors that, again, made me confident that it was the place for me. Throughout college, I cherished the memory of that trip.

Amy taught me about courage – last spring, she conquered her fear of flying, which arose because of a helicopter crash, and flew out to visit our dad in California. On that trip she made me promise to conquer my own fear of swimming. Last Tuesday night, I went swimming. I swam 6 laps (a personal record) and I was so proud I did it – and even more proud that I kept my promise to her. I meant to call her Wednesday, but it was too late in the evening. But I believe she knows.

Amy also taught me about grief. She had lost so many friends and relatives – she taught me that by loving and caring deeply, you always ache deeply when you lose people. She is teaching me that now.

But, by example, she also taught me to keep on loving – and saying I love you. Amy always said "I love you." As my mother said yesterday – Amy was a great lover. I think loving may truly be Amy's greatest talent.

Afterword

Since I wrote this, I continue to have what I call "Amy Moments" – the times when I see her in my life. The best example is an awful day at work when I had been gruffly sent to a conference room to get something done – and in trouble that it was not already done – while everyone else attended the meeting. Wanting to quit or cry, my bag lunch arrived – and what was sitting on top? Fritos. Clearly a gift of encouragement from Amy, I opened the bag, went to look out of the window, shed a few tears, ate my Fritos and thanked her for being there for me. I got what I had to do done with greater confidence and went back to the meeting.

Amanda's story shows the love between two sisters and the pedestal that younger siblings sometimes put their older siblings on. Thinking back to my younger brother Ray, who died in 1992, he did the same thing. Only I didn't realize the influence I had on him then and I didn't always make good decisions. Amy knew exactly what influence she had, and was a wonderful example for her sister. I couldn't help but recognize that such a small thing like a bag of Fritos could turn someone's day completely around.

I particularly enjoyed Amanda's phrase for times when she sees or thinks of Amy in her life..."Amy Moments." I have "Grampy Moments" all the time. He died in 1985, and sometimes, even now, I'll be in a public place and will start to cry when I remember something we did together or something he said. Grief doesn't really go away, it just subsides to where we can bear it. I take solace in the fact that I have so many memories, as I'm sure Amanda does. These "Moments" last a lifetime and, even when they make me cry, are a good thing.

Amy was a special person to so many people. Her husband Chuck was the one who knew her best and describes her in the following excerpts from his story entitled, "My Princess".

> Amy and I met as freshmen as the University of New Hampshire...[and] became very good friends that second semester. Then, in June of 1981, after Amy and I had not seen each other in about a month, she called to say...maybe we could get together. We [did, and] at the end of the night I kissed her. Not the "friend kiss" we had so often given each other, but a passionate one.
>
> We [fell] in love that summer and my life would never be the same. I was in love with a dancer full of boundless energy and spontaneity. We used to go dancing [and] I could see the music in her movements. Over the months...we realized we completed each other.
>
> We said our vows on June 23, 1984. She always kidded about marrying Prince Charles. She loved the Royals and especially Princess Diana. So after the wedding she became my princess.
>
> We both graduated college and had started building our house. I, being a country boy, was determined to participate in the construction process. Amy agreed to help, [and] we started by clearing the land for the driveway. Now you must picture a city girl, a ballerina, my princess, in knee-deep snow learning how to take the limbs off the trees I was cutting down with a chainsaw. She learned to "limb-up" like a pro. She also took over the job of construction supervisor (informally of course) and...she finished lumber before the builder nailed it in place. She put so much of herself into our house it truly became a home filled with love.

She had always lived in the city and wasn't used to the distances between the houses. To quote, "I can't see any of the other houses, are you sure this is safe?" Now jump ahead two years and neighbors are building next to our house in what was a horse pasture. She told me if any more houses were built close to us, we would have to move further north to avoid the sprawl. My princess was now a country girl.

We became one with our little piece of Earth. Amy found she loved to garden [and] she excelled in nurturing young plants.

Animals were naturally drawn to her and she to them. She could also talk with them. During a fundraising event at someone's home, one of the horses the family owned [came] to the door to join the party. Amy intercepted the horse and politely told him he would have to go back to the pasture and she would see him later. He turned around and strolled back to the pasture. After the event was over she started off for her car, walking along the fence line. The horse came to greet her [and] she asked if he would like to walk her down to her car. He whinnied and walked next to her until she said her goodbyes at the car. He then turned and galloped back to the barn.

She used her fundraising experience to help an animal welfare group raise funds for their various campaigns. As a thank you for our donation and fundraising efforts we were invited to Prince Edward Island in March 1991 for a trip on the pack ice to visit the Harp seal pups. These are the adorable white pups born each February and March in the Gulf of St. Lawrence, Canada. Amy and I reveled in the beauty of the ice and little seals. We even got to snuggle one well-fed and content pup.

After doing this once, we wanted more...the following year we went to visit the seals again [and] vowed to make this an annual pilgrimage. The third year...the weather was not cooperating. The helicopters had been grounded for four days due to poor visibility. On the last day of our stay, the overcast had lifted and the sky looked much brighter, [so] we flew north [and] after 45 minutes, we heard the pilot of the helicopter behind us urgently instructing our pilot to "pull up, pull up". A split second later we crashed into the pack ice.

Our injuries were not life threatening, but they were serious enough. Amy had suffered injuries to her neck and back that required 18 months of physical therapy and I had five months of therapy. We never fully recovered from these injuries. My lingering problems are minor. Amy was not so fortunate. In the last couple of years, she endured daily pain.

The accident strengthened her love and zest for life. We didn't look at the world in the same way. Daily annoyances just didn't carry the same weight. Our love for friends and family became stronger and more important. Our love for each other was also strengthened. We spent more time together. We were much more willing to take on new challenges. In my case, with a lot of encouragement and support from Amy, I started my own consulting business. For Amy, the challenge was more personal.

She always had dreamed of being an Olympic athlete, but dance had never been an Olympic sport. Then, during the 1996 Atlanta Olympic Games, we were watching the archery competition and Amy announced, "Now that I can do!" For the next few years she faithfully practiced and with encouragement from her coach, truly thought she might have a chance of trying for the Olympic team. Her injuries forced her to put down the bow, but not before she retired as the Women's Novice Champion for New Hampshire.

Amy was a storyteller, both with spoken and written word. The way she embellished her stories made everyday events seem like wonderful adventures. This gift could also have some drawbacks however. Phone bills come to mind. Many people tried to get her to be a writer, including myself. She never got to be that writer so this book, which includes her story, is a fitting tribute to such a fine storyteller.

Whether it was making fun of a character on "General Hospital" or building a snowcat (not snowman) in our yard, or dancing down the streets of New York signing "42nd Street", we let ourselves be kids. One of the things I loved about Amy was the way she made up names for people and animals. Our neighbor's pig Anikin (Skywalker) – with whom Amy had a bit of a love affair with – earned the moniker "Darth Pigger". It is her humor that I think I miss the most. Even when one of us was having a bad day, the other would usually do or say something silly and whatever the problem, it didn't seem as serious.

What I have written here only begins to illustrate the beautiful, wonderful, complex person that was Amy Alice Monchamp Huckins. She was a dedicated worker, a volunteer, a caretaker of animals, a steward of the Earth, a sister, a daughter, an aunt, a Godmother, a friend to all, an angel to many, my best friend, my soul mate, my wife and always and forever, my princess.

After Amy's death I struggled with the question of why she was taken from all of us. My thoughts keep coming back to something her friend Kristi told me after the accident. She said, "God needed an angel that he did not have to train."

What struck me the most during my time with Amy's family was the way each person described Amy as always happy. In fact, in every picture I saw of her, she had a huge smile. Her eyes seemed to twinkle with joy. I asked Chuck how Amy reacted when she got mad, and he told me she never really got mad. Sounds like an angel to me.

Amy's mom, Allie, had this to say:

"As a little kid, Amy had a sense of wonder about the world that never left her. Everything was exciting – a big deal! "You're not going to believe it!" Same attitude when telling about making friends with a new girl in first grade; her solo ballet at the Palace Theatre; seeing a mouse escape from the cat; falling in love with Chuck; being awarded a scholarship; picking out a Halloween pumpkin. Wow – what a world – one big adventure – that's how she viewed life.

Even bad things that happened were part of the big adventure. A helicopter crash, back and knee problems..."You're not going to believe how nice my doctor is."

I never heard Amy say she was bored. Too much happening – wild turkeys spotted in the yard; new book to read; new political campaign to work on; a doctor's visit; squirrels to be fed (yes, fed!). Nobody had to tell Amy to stop and smell the roses.

At the wake and the reception after the funeral, people who had never met were laughing about how they knew everything about each other through Amy. She thought everything about everyone was interesting and needed to be communicated to everyone else. That telephone! Now we're trying to deal with no more phone calls – no more Amy's voice.

Yes, she was "beloved". I've never seen so many heartbroken women as her friends were at her wake. So many people considered her their best friend. She had a wonderful way of making people feel good about themselves and letting them know she thought they were special.

At the wake one of her old high school friends was recalling to me how back in those days when she was getting involved with drugs, Amy was the only one of the "good" kids who stood by her. Her friends said to me, "If it weren't for Amy, I wouldn't be alive today."

So now we're facing life without Amy. No Amy who, along about August, would be talking about Christmas plans — homemade cards, hundreds of wonderful homemade cookies (what she called "cookie brigade") and what she was buying or making for Christmas gifts.

The thing is, Amy shared with us her wonder about the world. She brightened so many lives, certainly mine. I will always miss the light.

Everything in life was a big deal in an exciting and enthusiastic way. Amy Huckins truly "lived" life. If you were around her, you had no choice but to "live" life as well. Her spirit and attitude were contagious. Knowing Amy would have been great therapy when I got depressed.

She was involved in so many different facets of life, one could hardly keep up. She worked for many political campaigns and causes, including former New Hampshire State Representative and Senator, Wayne King. They became close during this time and Wayne remembers Amy this way:

As I sit to write this tribute to Amy Huckins, a thousand images overwhelm my soul and I find it very hard to focus. Perhaps it is because these feelings are a reflection of Amy herself...so filled with energy and enthusiasm; exalting in life and living it every single day.

Besides my parents, Amy and Chuck were the first people to whom Alice and I entrusted our precious 3 year-old, Zach, for an evening. Zach returned to us safe and sound, bearing photos of he and Amy parading around the kitchen wearing colanders on their heads...playing the part of domestic knights defending the kitchen from all enemies. Later visits to "Auntie" Amy yielded photos of the longest bathtub spit I have ever witnessed and a myriad of other glimpses into both my son and Amy's inner child.

With Amy, the inner child was always percolating just below the surface. A consummate professional in her roles...anyone who came to know her understood quickly that the gleam in her eye came from the fact that, even in the most serious of moments, that child yearned to leap out and surprise you.

...Even within the less than gentle circle of life in the animal kingdom, Amy was always attempting to calm the turbulent waters. When Amy saw a coyote in her backyard representing a threat to her beloved cat Emily, her response was to make Chuck pee in a jar for weeks and "mark" the territory along the stone wall and the rest of the property to ward off the predator. She would have fought to the end to protect her Emily, but she would brook no threat to the life of an animal that was only doing what nature intended.

Living gently, but intensely, Amy touched the lives of so many of us. Her life was far too short but her spirit will carry on in those of us who loved her. When Zach grows to teach his own son the finer points of culinary knighthood or the art of the tubspit, I suspect Amy's spirit will be right there laughing and cheering him on.

Here is her older sister, Lisa's, account of special times with Amy:

Amy had the most graceful arms and hands – like a swan. One of my favorite memories is watching her perform a jazz dance...she loved the stage and had a dramatic flair.

Amy was the most generous and caring person I have ever known. Several times in our adult lives I had surgery and my sister would do whatever needed to be done: laundry, cooking, dishes and help with my boys. I sometimes think it's ironic that I became the nurse in the family because Amy was the one who came to the rescue. If you were sick or "down for the count," Amy would be there.

I am flooded with memories of her laughter, her kindness and our secrets. Sometimes they are a source of comfort to me and sometimes they are a painful reminder of what I have lost.

It's always painful to know we will never see our loved ones on earth again. I wonder which is worse, not knowing the person in the first place (and not receiving the blessings of knowing them) or knowing and enjoying them for a time, only to lose them forever.

In the end, what do we really have? Is it important to have a wake and a funeral? Or should we simply remember the person the way we knew them in life? Amy's friend Ron Burnette, who performed in many shows with Amy and eventually formed his own production company, answers these questions poignantly.

Her wake was six hours away, and I didn't know if twelve hours of driving would be worth it. Chancing it, we made the drive. In a hot room with a thousand people and a hundred floral arrangements and a long, long line to meet the family, I found a single arrangement with a simple card bearing "urchins forever". Her friend Bonnie was frequently in shows with Amy and me, and one was "Roar of the Greasepaint". Amy played an "urchin," as did Bonnie and 12 other girls. All those shows, one after the other, college, summer stock, I had wondered for years; had it meant anything to anyone? Here, twenty years later, at the wake of my little Amy, Bonnie had sent flowers bearing "urchins forever". It mattered.

I am not an urchin. I was the lead of the show, and I thought far too much of myself in those days to be an urchin, so I can't rightly claim urchin status now. But I did really know an urchin, really loved an urchin, and know she loved me, too. And once loved by an urchin, well, life is never really the same, is it?

Although I knew Amy only in death, she taught me many lessons: that giving is so much more rewarding than receiving; and that a small amount of creativity is enough to make memories last forever. I've learned to make small things a big deal. Most of all though, I've learned that happiness can only come from within. Regardless of the curve balls life may throw at me, it's my choice how I react.

Sunshine on My Shoulders

The Story of Brooke Elizabeth Blanchard
1978 – 1996

"Those who bring sunshine to the lives of others cannot keep it from themselves."
James Barrie

EVERY FAMILY I serve touches my heart in one form or another. When funeral service is a passion, that's just the way it is. As with anything in life, some situations stand out in your mind and will be ingrained in your memory forever. Such was the case with 17-year old Brooke Blanchard.

Bob Bennett called me and gave me instructions to go to Concord Hospital and bring back Brooke. He told me she was a 17-year old soccer star who had been killed while riding in a car with a drunk driver — while she had no alcohol in her at all. I vividly recall every moment of that day, and many moments of the days to follow.

Having a daughter just two years younger than Brooke made this more personal somehow: I was filled with anger, fear, sadness, and a sense of helplessness for her family. I asked God, out loud, why this had to happen. Still, I tried to put my feelings aside because I had a job to do. I soon learned Brooke's mother, Ginger, wanted to see her daughter, *before* a casket had been chosen.

I toiled for what seemed like eternity in the preparation room of the funeral home. Embalming was one thing, but trying to create the memory picture I wanted for the family was a different story altogether. One can only imagine the physical trauma which occurs in high speed crashes. Even so, Ginger expected to see Brooke that day.

Because a casket had yet to be selected, I placed Brooke's clean and completely dressed, but lifeless, body on a dressing table so her family could see her. When her mom entered the back of the room and saw her beautiful child laying dead on the table, she began screaming in disbelief and eventually passed out right where she was standing. Mr. Bennett remained in the room with Ginger, and I stayed in the doorway with Brooke's brothers, John and Andrew. Her youngest brother, Andrew (13 at the time), who was holding a teddy bear, tugged at my jacket and pointed to the girl on the table saying, "That's my sister. Can she have this teddy bear?" I reached out as he was handing me the bear and, without knowing it would happen, I began to cry. Even though Mr. Bennett insisted we were there to serve families and not mingle tears with them, I don't regret showing my feelings. I know I did my job well, regardless of my emotions.

Brooke's dad, Steve, who was also very close to his daughter, sat in another room, looking off into the distance with a blank stare, almost as if he didn't know where he was. I couldn't begin to grasp the pain that he, Ginger, and Brooke's brothers were experiencing. As I wiped away my tears, all I knew was that the one place I didn't want to be, was there.

Brooke was more than a typical high school girl. In her sophomore year, she was her high school soccer team's MVP. She was also a member of the Concord Bible Fellowship and the Hopkinton High School peer outreach program. In fact, she made it a point to befriend those less fortunate than she. Dr. Ralph and Pat Beasley wrote this letter to Brooke's parents shortly after she died:

Dear Ginger & Steven,

Brooke was a wonderful child and we will remember her in ways and for reasons that you are probably not even aware of.

Our daughter Meredith, who is the age of most sophomores, is autistic. Two years ago when Meredith came back to public schools in Hopkinton, Brooke was her peer tutor. Meredith was so overwhelmed with everything about school that she was almost in a shut down mode. After January of that year, Brooke met with

Meredith every day to help her work on English. Brooke was kind, gentle, and funny, when she worked with Meredith. Meredith was having such a difficult time; kids were making fun of her or totally ignoring her. She frequently talked to no other student during the course of the day.

Meredith began to work again, in great part because of Brooke. She would tell us the funny things that Brooke would say. Brooke gave her warmth and companionship when no one else would. We can't tell you how much the time she spent with Meredith meant to us. Brooke became the one and only constant in Meredith's life that year. She was assigned to take Meredith as a student, but she went far beyond any obligation of simple teaching, and reached out to a sometimes difficult, very troubled child. I'm not sure Meredith would have been able to continue had it not been for people like Brooke.

We will always be grateful to Brooke, and I know Meredith will always remember her as a kind, helping, and friendly girl.

Not only did she make an impression on other students, but her teachers were touched by her sunny personality as well, as evidenced in this letter from teacher, Harry Zottos:

Dear Mr. & Mrs. Blanchard,

You probably don't know me, but I knew Brooke while substitute teaching at Hopkinton H.S. last spring.

I met Brooke my first day of teaching there in a foreign language class. At first, Brooke surprised me by insisting on knowing my first name while I was trying to settle the class. I tried to brush her off by avoiding her, but she and her friends spent almost the entire period guessing my name and saying practically every name known on earth! Not remembering her name on my first day, I inadvertently called her Bonnie for some reason and she broke out laughing with her friends. After the days went by, she would often bring that up that I called her Bonnie instead of Brooke, and it became a joke between us.

After getting to know Brooke, I was very impressed with her personality, and especially how she treated others. Whenever I saw Brooke at school or at a game, she would say hello to me or come up and talk to me. One thing I remember is when I was driving in from Manchester Brooke would pass me in her caravan going in the opposite direction bringing her little brother to school.

Brooke would wave to me as I passed. Not many young people have the kindness and politeness Brooke possessed.

As I sit here and look at the write-up I become very upset. I think of all the mean and hateful people in the world and wonder why someone like Brooke had to have this happen. I can recall the funny faces Brooke would make at me when I would joke with her and she and her friends would innocently tease me in class.

I only knew her for a short period so I can't even begin to imagine how you and your family feel. I'm sorry for your loss.

Brooke was very close to her family. As a soccer player she wore jersey # 17. After her death, both of Brooke's brothers and her cousins all wore #17 for their respective teams in soccer, baseball, and other sports. It was their way of honoring Brooke and of keeping her memory alive. For her part, Brooke's mother, Ginger, is a tireless volunteer for MADD (Mothers Against Drunk Driving).

For a mother to lose her only daughter just as she's blossoming into a woman, is devastating. Ginger wrote these thoughts in a letter to Brooke, seven years after Brooke's death:

Brooke,

I wonder if you were afraid, if you knew for those seconds before the crash if you were going to die. To think you were in a car with a drunk driver, you weren't even drinking, and yet, you were the one that died. I was at work when I got the phone call from dad. I remember thinking, "I will never be the mother of the bride." After the state trooper arrived and told me you were gone, all I wanted to do was see you and hold you, but I couldn't get to you. I just wanted to make sure you had a blanket so you wouldn't get cold.

When we were picking out your clothes, I made sure you had your purple rag wool socks and your khaki pants and red sweater I bought you for Christmas. When I did see you, you looked so perfect. I couldn't believe what was happening. The day you died, Brooke, I died with you, only my heart didn't stop beating.

How do you say goodbye? How do you stop the hurt from hurting? How do you get through another holiday? There were so many things we didn't get to do. I wanted to teach you how to cook special things and how to start traditions to bring with you to your family.

I still struggle to deal with your death, but I make sure people remember you as you lived. You were confident, artistic, and your heart was so big. As a speaker for MADD-NH and VICTIMS, Inc. I want others to learn from you. It's through you teaching me to die, that I can teach others to live. I am so proud of the young woman you became, and in your death, I'm proud of the difference you continue to make. I miss and love you very much.

MOM

Brooke was a special daughter. She was also a loyal and honest friend, even when she was 12 years old. Her friend, Cheryl Dombrowski, tells this story which shows what honesty and friendships are all about:

Brooke and Pancakes

True honesty is hard to find in some people, but when you had a friend like Brooke, it was something that you knew came with the territory. She never had any trouble telling others how she felt and you knew that whatever she said was exactly what she meant.

The morning after one of our weekly twelve-year-old sleepovers provided me with a valuable tool that I have taken with me throughout my life. I decided that I was going to make her pancakes, using the "secret" recipe that I had learned from my dad. I mixed all the correct ingredients to the precise measurements I had written down earlier, and made sure that I sprayed the non-stick pan with non-stick spray, just to make sure that the pancakes would come out perfectly. As I began to ladle the batter into the pan, I noticed that the batter was spreading a little bit faster than I remembered when my dad made them, but I continued anyway thinking that I was still doing it right. When they were cooked "to a golden brown" I took them off the pan and arranged them on a plate in a beautiful display. Brooke put her usual butter and syrup on them and began to eat.

As I watched her eat the first couple of bites, I was a little confused by the expression on her face. Finally after the third bite she said to me, "Cheryl, they are so gross, I think they are raw." At first I was a little taken by her, thinking she was being mean, but waited to listen to what she had to say. She continued to tell me that they probably are really good, but that she had to teach me how to cook them. Apparently I was not supposed to put the burner on high. I thought it would just make them cook faster, but as I listened to Brooke tell me I had to cook them slowly, I realized what I had done wrong. She cooked another batch, showing me the correct temperature that I needed the burner to be at, and of course, they came out perfect.

I learned a valuable lesson that morning. When you have a friend as close as Brooke, trust what they say to you. I was almost upset that Brooke did not like my pancakes, but when I realized that she wanted to help, I knew that she was not being honest to be unkind, but to help me improve. Although it was something as small as making pancakes, it was her honesty about them that was important. She taught me that it's okay to be that honest with a friend. Friends need that in each other to help them learn and grow into the true person that we want them to be.

Mimi Harper summed up her feelings toward Brooke this way:

"To know Brooke was to love her, and I did. You knew when she loved you too. I got a hug and a nice greeting each time we saw each other. Her death has filled me with pain I have not felt since my son died."

There is no rhyme or reason to this thing we call death. We will never even begin to understand why things like this happen to such beautiful and promising lives. We can however, take the lessons learned from these tragedies and implement them in our daily living.

We are each allotted only so much time to do whatever it is God wants us to accomplish. Since we do not know what that time frame is, I think it wise to cherish what we have now and make every moment in our life last.

Looking at Brooke's bright and shining smile reminds me of a radiant sunshine which she spread everywhere she went. Now, when I feel the sunshine on my shoulders, I am easily reminded of Brooke and the happiness she shared when she was alive. May 4, 2003 would have been her 25th birthday. Would she have been a college graduate? Would she have played soccer with Mia Hamm on the U.S. Women's team? Perhaps she'd be married and have a child of her own. But for the senseless act of one man driving under the influence of alcohol, while under age, we'll never know. One thing I do know: Brooke's life had meaning and purpose, and for the 17 years she lived, she made her mark on the world and continues to do so through her mother's efforts in MADD.

Don't let your life just pass you by. Make every moment count and be the "Sunshine" Brooke so exemplified. There are people in the world today well into their seventies and eighties who, by their own choosing, have not lived fulfilling lives. It's never too late to start. Brooke's story helped me to realize the importance of everyday when I was still in my thirties. So, whether you are 15 or 95, know it's never too late, and in the words of John Denver, "If I had a wish that I could wish for you, I'd make a wish that sun shines all the while."

Epilogue

I hope this book has touched your heart. I wrote it with the intention of not only keeping the memory of some fabulous people alive, but to show all who read it how each and every one of us have the potential to make an impact in this world.

When I first began this project, I got the usual naysayers telling me there are millions of people exactly like those in this book, and therefore it would be nothing special.

I am happy to agree there are, in fact, millions of people making a huge difference in their world. That's *exactly* what makes this book special. Our heroes are in our own backyards. There is no need to look for "famous" people to idolize.

We all struggle to keep pace with the rest of the world, sometimes forgetting to stop and look around at the people and things closest to us. Let us not forget how short life can be and always remember to appreciate what we have. Your life counts.

— Eric Daniels

"Somewhere out there is a unique place for you to help others—
a unique life role for you that only you can fill."

Thomas Kinkade

About the Author

AFTER SERVING IN the U.S. Army as a Paratrooper, Eric Daniels studied Funeral Science, winning recognition and highest honors during his schooling. He became a Funeral Director in 1995, and has worked in Funeral Homes in New Hampshire, Pennsylvania, and Florida.

Mr. Daniels has published articles in newspapers and trade magazines, and is active in his community with several service clubs and helping students with high school sports. He is also a member of the New Hampshire House of Representatives.

He and his wife, Kelly, live in Concord, New Hampshire with eight children: Jessica, Stefanie, Joseph, Ashley, and Megan; nephews Matt and Josh; and one grandchild, Isabella.

The author can be reached at:
The Greatest People
c/o Eric Daniels
5 Flume St.
Concord, NH 03303

ilwed@aol.com

Printed in the United States
46603LVS00007B/112-135